CANADA'S
CONSTITUTIONAL
CRISIS

Making Sense of It All
(A Background Analysis & A Look at the Future)

BY
MARJORIE
BOWKER
C.M./B.A./LL.B./LL.D.

LONE
PINE

The publisher:
Lone Pine Publishing
206, 10426-81 Avenue
Edmonton, Alberta, Canada
T6E 1X5

Canadian Cataloguing in Publishing Data

Bowker, Marjorie Montgomery
    Canada's Constitutional Crisis

ISBN 1-55105-002-1
    1. Canada—Constitutional law—Amendments. 2. Canada—Constitutional history. 3. Federal government—Canada. 4. Federal—provincial relations—Canada
I. Title.
JL65.1991 B68 1991   342.71'03   C91-091660-8

Front cover: Horst H. Krause, Will Jang
Layout and design: Beata Kurpinski
Editorial: Elaine Butler, Gary Whyte
Printing: Quality Printing Ltd., Edmonton, Alberta, Canada

The publisher gratefully acknowledges the assistance of the Federal Department of Communications, Alberta Culture and Multiculturalism, the Canada Council, and the Alberta Foundation for the Literary Arts in the production of this book.

Dedicated to my seven grandchildren and
to all the children of this favoured land

TABLE OF CONTENTS

ACKNOWLEDGEMENTS

I wish to especially thank Professor Gerald L. Gall of the Faculty of Law, University of Alberta, for his meticulous reading of my draft; also Cheryl Robison for transcribing my manuscript; Grant Kennedy, President of Lone Pine Publishing, for his encouragement and enthusiasm; and most of all my husband, Wilbur F. Bowker, O.C., Q.C., who after 50 years of marriage is still my favourite mentor.

- MARJORIE BOWKER

FOREWORD

The challenge facing Canadians is no less than the preservation of our country. We are now engaged in restructuring our Constitution. We must prepare ourselves to become participants in this process by an intelligent understanding of the issues.

The Canadian Constitution is both complex and exciting. It has its roots in some 200 years of history. It belongs to all of us, as does the course of future change.

If there were ever a time when our nation needed an informed and educated population — alert to the risk, yet aware of the possibilities — that time is NOW.

The purpose of this book is to assist the general public in understanding the Constitution and its historical background — to enable all Canadians to follow events and formulate their own views. We must bring to the process tolerance, flexibility, reasonableness and sensitivity.

Nation-building requires vision and insight. This is the era of populism — the doctrine of citizen empowerment — the belief that individuals can make a difference.

MARJORIE MONTGOMERY BOWKER
C.M., B.A., LL.B., LL.D.
Former Judge
Provincial Court of Alberta
Family and Juvenile Divisions
(1966-1983)

Edmonton, Alberta
August 10, 1991.

1
ROOTS OF THE CANADIAN CONSTITUTION

"Constitutional convention plus constitutional law equal the total constitution of the country." With these words, the Supreme Court of Canada in 1981 described the ingredients of Canada's Constitution. In its broadest sense, constitution means the framework of government, the basic law of the land.

BACKGROUND HISTORY

The structure of Canada's Constitution is founded in our historic roots and can best be understood by examining our evolution as a nation.

Aboriginal peoples were the first inhabitants of what is now Canada. The first European settlers were the French. Early Canada was a French colony (New France) for some 150 years until the British conquest in 1759 following the Battle of the Plains of Abraham.

The Royal Proclamation of 1763 established English rule and a constitutional framework for negotiating native treaties. As early as 1774 under British rule, the Québec Act gave recognition to the French civil law, which prevails in Québec to this day. The Constitutional Act of 1791 created Upper and Lower Canada (portions of modern-day Ontario and Québec), and assured the beginnings of the British parliamentary system. The Act of Union of 1840, which reunited the two provinces, launched the transition from a British colony to a self-governing nation and established a basis for responsible government. This is the principle where the Executive (or Cabinet) is responsible to the Legislature, a fundamental feature of our present parliamentary structure.

THE FEDERAL SYSTEM

All of these historical events constitute the backdrop for Canada's federal system. By federalism we mean a political system where power to make laws is divided between a central (or federal) government and a number of provinces (or states). Other federations, besides Canada, are Australia and the United States, each having a national government and several state governments. By way of contrast, Great Britain and New Zealand have a unitary form of government where all legislative power is vested in one central government. Canada must forever remain a federal system as it is too vast and diverse to be under the authority of a single jurisdiction.

Canadian federalism had its beginnings in the British North America Act of 1867, now renamed the Constitution Act 1867. To this day it remains a central component of Canada's Constitution.

THE BRITISH NORTH AMERICA ACT 1867
(RENAMED THE CONSTITUTION ACT 1867)

The BNA Act was enacted by the British Parliament in 1867 at the request of Canadian political leaders. It was the result of some three years of discussion, consultations and conferences, beginning with the Charlottetown conference of 1864, followed later by conferences in Québec City and London, England.

The Act provided for a confederation of four provinces — Nova Scotia, New Brunswick, and the Union of Upper and Lower Canada (representing portions of present-day Ontario and Québec) — with a parliamentary system modelled on that of Britain. To the original four provinces, six more were added later: Manitoba (1870); British Columbia (1871); Prince Edward Island (1873); Alberta and Saskatchewan (1905); Newfoundland (1949). The North West Territories and the Yukon remain "Territories," not having yet attained provincial status.

The BNA Act provides for the division of legislative (law-making) powers as between the federal and provincial governments. The broadest powers are vested in the federal government, comprising 29 subjects (section 91) including: trade and commerce, militia and defence, the postal service, census and statistics, navigation and shipping, transportation and communication, fisheries, banking, currency, interest, criminal law, bankruptcy, copyrights, Indians, divorce, and the general power of "peace, order and good government." Provincial legislative powers are enumerated in section 92, comprising 16 subjects, including: property and civil rights, solemnization of marriage, administration of justice, local works and undertakings, hospital maintenance, municipal government, and "generally all matters of a merely local and private nature in the province."

Where there is conflict in jurisdiction between provincial and federal fields, the federal power prevails (this is the so-called paramountcy rule). There are two areas — agriculture and immigration — where the two orders of government have concurrent jurisdiction (section 95).

Generally speaking, the BNA Act as a whole is a centralist document favouring strength at the federal level.

A key challenge in the current constitutional debate will be a restructuring of the division of powers between the federal and provincial governments with strong pressure from Québec for decentralization with vastly increased provincial powers, and reduced powers in the central government.

Historically, the Fathers of Confederation perceived the need for a strong central government, in contrast to the American Constitution formulated almost a century earlier (1789) in which the residuary power was given to the states. In 1867 when the BNA Act was being formulated, the American Civil War had just been fought. Sir John A. Macdonald, the Canadian Prime Minister at the time, spoke strongly in favour of a strong central government for Canada, which if it had existed in the United States, in his opinion, could have prevented an insurrection by the states leading to Civil War. Now, over a century later, Canada might draw a parallel as to the need for strong central leadership

Other provisions of the BNA Act which remain basic to our Constitution are:

◆ the composition, structure and powers of the House of Commons;

◆ the role of the Senate and qualification of Senators;

◆ the functioning of the Judicial system;

◆ the establishment of the provincial legislatures;

◆ the role of the Governor-General and Lieutenant Governors;

◆ education including the right of separate schools in some provinces;

◆ revenue, debts, assets and taxation;

◆ numerous miscellaneous provisions.

to prevent the possible dismemberment of the country. With its vast geographical area and small scattered population, Canada has over the years needed a strong federal government to attain the level of unity which it has achieved.

The BNA Act itself has been the subject of amendments over the years — though surprisingly few major ones, considering the lapse of more than a century. These amendments were all incorporated into the Act, and until 1982, only the British Parliament was empowered to make amendments — which were done of course only at the request of the Canadian Parliament.

Not only is the Act itself a key part of our Canadian Constitution, so also are the hundreds of judicial decisions over the decades involving the legal interpretation of its various sections. Many significant landmark decisions were rendered by the Judicial Committee of the Privy Council in London, England, during the period up to 1949 when it was the final court of appeal for Canada. Thereafter that role shifted to the Supreme Court of Canada.[1]

The foregoing demonstrates the essential fusion between statute law, which is "written" (such as the BNA Act), and the "unwritten" case law comprising legal precedents laid down through court decisions. These are the two main ingredients of the Canadian Constitution.

There is a third, though less important component, called "convention," which refers to vaguely-defined customs and usages — those which, through consistent application over a period of time, have acquired constitutional status. Examples are: parliamentary supremacy, responsibility of Cabinet to Parliament and the use of executive power within the political context.

Thus, in summary, the three components of our Constitution are: written statutes, unwritten case law, and convention.

---

[1] Since 1975, before launching an appeal to the Supreme Court, it has been necessary to obtain permission from that Court to do so (except in very limited fields). In actual fact, permission is not often granted, with the result that the Courts of Appeal for the various provinces have become virtually the final court for most litigants.

STATUTE OF WESTMINSTER 1931

In respect to international relations, reference should be made to the Statute of Westminster (1931), which too was an Act of the British Parliament. The Act is important in that it transferred to Canada full control over foreign affairs, a role previously exercised by Britain. This meant, for example, that in World War II, Canada made its own declaration of war — the declaration by Britain did not automatically bind Canada. It has also meant that Canada could have its own Citizenship Act (1947) and its own flag (1965) replacing the Union Jack. Appropriately, the British monarch is now described as the Queen of Canada.

2
THE CONSTITUTION ACT 1982

EARLY EFFORTS AT REFORM

For 115 years (1867 to 1982) Canada's only major constitutional statute was the BNA Act of 1867 (and amendments). During all these years, the power to amend the constitution rested with the British Parliament. This was not because Britain wished to retain the amending power, but rather that the federal and provincial governments could not agree on an alternative method of amendment. At Canada's request, a special section had been included in the Statute of Westminster (section 7) by which the amending power was to remain in the British Parliament.

During a period of over 50 years (1927 to 1981) there were at least ten rounds of negotiations in an attempt to reach agreement on a new Canadian Constitution, including a formula for amending it. One of the earliest studies on the distribution of legislative powers was the Rowell-Sirois Report in 1940, though few of its recommendations were implemented.

On the subject of the amending process, in 1964 the federal and provincial governments endorsed a complicated procedure — the so-called Fulton-Favreau formula (an amended version of the 1960 Fulton formula). However, in 1965, Québec Premier Lesage withdrew his endorsement of this proposal.

Perhaps the most encouraging attempt at constitutional reform occurred in 1971 when all ten provinces and the federal government endorsed the "Victoria Charter" which was really a new constitution. Within a few days after it was signed, however, the government of Québec (Robert Bourassa being then in his earlier term as Premier) revoked Québec's previous approval, alleging that the Province's interests had not been sufficiently protected.

Still another attempt at amendment was made in 1979, resulting in the Pepin-Robarts formula. It advocated ratification of constitutional amendments by a national referendum, requiring majority approval by each of four regions.

During 1978–1979, the most extensive series of conferences which had been held to that date on constitutional reform were convened by then Prime Minister Pierre Trudeau. Discussions took place over a period of some 17 months. Fourteen items were presented for review, including subjects such as: division of powers, patriation of the Constitution, an amending formula, human rights, divorce, Senate reform and the Supreme Court. The meetings ended in acrimony with no agreement reached. Nonetheless, the material presented, and the records of debates on the 14 items, might serve as a useful guide today.[2]

From this review, it is obvious that attempts at constitutional reform have been going on in Canada for years, with little awareness on the part of the Canadian public. However by the late 1970s, Québec was becoming increasingly dissatisfied with the slowness of change, and in May 1980 its government held a referendum on sovereignty association. The defeat of the resolution was due in large part to the undertaking by Mr. Trudeau to immediately address Québec's concerns.

EVENTS LEADING TO
THE CONSTITUTION ACT 1982

Following the defeat of the Québec referendum on sovereignty in 1980, the federal government under Prime Minister Trudeau began at once to negotiate with the provinces for constitutional change. There were three objectives: to deal with the Québec issue; to agree on an amending process so as to remove the need for British Parliamentary approval; and to enact a Charter of Rights and Freedoms (a long-standing dream of Prime Minister Trudeau).

On all of these issues there was discord and controversy. Provincial premiers blocked negotiations at every turn and eventually forced a reference to the Supreme Court of Canada on whether the federal government could proceed with its proposed constitutional changes without agreement from all provinces. At the time of the reference, only two provinces favoured the federal position. The decision of the Supreme Court was that although Ottawa had no legal duty to obtain

---

[2] Excellent coverage of these proceedings is contained in two issues of *Maclean's* magazine: February 19, 1979 and September 20, 1980.

agreement of all the provinces, *convention* dictated that there be at least a "consensus." This was interpreted to mean a "substantial number" of provinces — certainly greater than two but less than ten.[3]

It took some 18 months of meetings, conferences, proposals, revisions and compromises before sufficient consensus was reached, culminating in the new Constitution Act of 1982. In the end, it was endorsed by nine provincial premiers (some of them reluctantly), but not by Québec.

Much has been said about Québec being "excluded" from the Constitution Act of 1982. Actually Québec excluded itself, when its Premier, René Levesque, of his own volition refused to sign it. *Legally and constitutionally*, Québec is nonetheless a part of the Constitution.

When the Constitution came before the House of Commons for approval, the Québec Members of Parliament voted almost unanimously in its favour (only three being opposed). In addition, polls showed that a strong majority of Québec people supported the new Constitution. It is time we ended the myth (frequently publicized by Prime Minister Mulroney) that Québec was "betrayed, rejected and excluded" from the 1982 Constitution, when in truth it was Québec's own government which chose that position.

To this day, the government of Québec has not signed the Constitution Act of 1982. The Meech Lake Accord in 1990 was designed to obtain that signature, but failed.

Some light was shed on events during the period leading up to the 1982 Constitution, when on March 21, 1991, former Prime Minister Trudeau addressed the convocation at the University of Toronto on the occasion of receiving an honorary degree. He said that because the provincial premiers forced a reference to the Supreme Court, and because the Court ruled that the consent of a substantial number of provinces was needed, he as Prime Minister was forced to make inadvisable concessions to the provincial premiers in order to gain their approval, the effect of which was to weaken many aspects of the Constitution Act of 1982. This was particularly true of the amending procedure listing the subjects requiring unanimity. It led as well to the unfortunate addition of the override ("notwithstanding") clause in the Charter of Rights and Freedoms, allowing provinces to "opt out" of

---

[3]   *Re: Resolution to Amend the Constitution*, (1981) 1 S.C.R. 753.

particular provisions. If Mr. Trudeau had not agreed to these changes (much as he disapproved), the Act would never have passed and the original powers would have remained with the British Parliament.

CONSTITUTIONAL CHANGES IN 1982

The Constitution Act of 1982 was approved by the British Parliament (as was required at that time), and was signed in Ottawa by Her Majesty Queen Elizabeth II on behalf of Britain, and by Prime Minister Trudeau on behalf of Canada on April 17, 1982 — an occasion that has since been referred to as "Law Day."

The constitutional changes in 1982 consisted of two enactments:

Canada Act 1982

This was an Act of the British Parliament which did two things:

◆ it enacted our new Constitution (British approval still being necessary);

◆ It ended the British Parliament's function by transferring to the Canadian Parliament the power over future constitutional amendments, and Britain undertook never again to legislate in respect of Canada.

Constitution Act 1982

The Act is divided into seven Parts:

◆ Part I contains the Canadian Charter of Rights and Freedoms.

◆ Part II recognizes and affirms existing aboriginal and treaty rights of the aboriginal peoples of Canada.

◆ Part III deals with equal opportunities to all Canadians in respect to economic development and essential public services.

◆ Part IV provides for regular constitutional Conferences of First Ministers (the Prime Minister and provincial premiers), with aboriginal concerns included on the agenda.

◆ Part V deals with procedures for future amendments to the Constitution (the British Parliament no longer performing this role). There are two procedures governing future amendments:

• unanimity is required (that is, the agreement of the federal government and all provinces) regarding such matters as the following: the Office of the Queen, the Governor General and Lieutenant Governors; composition of the Supreme Court; structure of the House of Commons and Senate; the use of English and French.

• in regard to other matters, amendments can be made with the consent of the federal government plus two-thirds of the provinces representing 50 per cent of the population of Canada.

♦ Part VI confirms previous amendments.

♦ Part VII contains general provisions.

3

THE CANADIAN CHARTER OF RIGHTS AND FREEDOMS

As indicated above, the Charter constitutes the main part of the Constitution Act of 1982.

Its object is to protect Canadian citizens from violation of a vast range of rights and freedoms, including the following:

• freedom of conscience, religion, thought, belief, opinion and expression, including freedom of the press, as well as freedom of peaceful assembly and association;

• democratic rights, such as the right to vote;

• mobility rights — the right of citizens to enter or leave Canada, to move and earn a livelihood in other provinces;

• legal rights — including the right to life, liberty and security of the person; protection against unreasonable search and seizure, arbitrary imprisonment, arrest or detention; the right to counsel when charged, to habeas corpus, trial within a reasonable time; the presumption of innocence, right to a jury trial; protection from cruel and unusual punishment, right to an interpreter if required;

• equality rights — equality before the law, equal protection and equal benefit of the law without discrimination based on race, national or ethnic origin, colour, religion, sex, age or mental or physical disability;

• English and French the official languages, with provision for minority language educational rights.

The Charter contains as well several general provisions, including the preservation of Canada's multicultural heritage (section 27), and sexual equality rights for male and female persons (section 28). Perhaps the most important provision is section 52 which states that the Constitution of Canada is the supreme law of the country, and that any law which is inconsistent with it shall, to the extent of the inconsistency, be of no force and effect. This means that the courts can strike down as unconstitutional any statutes of Parliament, provincial

The theory behind the Charter is that it is designed to protect individuals against oppressive actions by the state (i.e., governments), whether it be in the form of an unfair law which fails to treat people equally; or in the form of unjust action by police in the arrest or detention of an accused; or a denial of rights in the course of a trial; or in the method of treatment and punishment.

legislatures or municipal governments which violate a right or freedom protected under the Charter. The same applies to any regulation, practice or procedure conducted pursuant to such statutes.

Thus the Charter represents a fundamental shift in philosophy as to legislative and judicial functions. Instead of Parliament and Legislatures having the paramount role in enacting laws, the Charter gives to the courts a new power to declare invalid any laws that contravene rights and liberties set out in the Charter. Whereas Parliament was formerly supreme, it is now the courts that have the last word. This means that the judiciary, consisting of appointed judges, become scrutinizers of legislatures (that is, elected representatives), in ensuring that the rights of citizens are protected.

Some persons contend that the Charter gives too much protection to criminals, and that charges are often dismissed on such grounds as: the accused not being allowed a lawyer or informed of the availability of legal aid; or the accused not being given protection against self-incrimination when questioned by police; or having too long a delay before trial. There have been times too where the courts have exercised their power to veto legislation when some people believe such legislation is justified. An instance of this (though corrected on appeal) occurred in Alberta when a lower court struck down as unconstitutional a law requiring the use of seat belts on the ground that it interfered with freedom of expression (which was interpreted to mean freedom of choice). During the long delay pending appeal, the validity of the seat belt legislation was in doubt and so was not being enforced by police, resulting (as statistics showed) in more accidents and deaths during that period. Instances such as this do unfortunately occur because all judges (including those in lower courts) have the power to strike down laws which, in their opinion, violate a right protected in the Charter. Until the ruling is clarified on appeal (often taking many months or as long as a year), it can have a "ripple effect" across Canada, leaving the law in doubt until the appeal is heard.

The Charter was also the basis on which Canada's abortion law was struck down in 1988, it being held by the Supreme Court of Canada that the restrictions imposed by the law on abortions violated the "security of the person" in respect to the rights of women.

Since 1982, when the Charter came into effect, thousands of cases have come before the courts in which the protection of the Charter has been raised as a defence. In the course of such cases, the courts have been called upon to define what the words of the Charter mean, and in the process the courts (ultimately the Supreme Court of Canada) have contributed a body of legal principles which become precedents for similar cases in future.

Since World War II there has been a trend in many countries (though not in Britain) to have rights protected in the Constitution. This is the first time Canada has entrenched such rights in its Constitution. The Charter differs from the Diefenbaker "Bill of Rights" of 1960 which was simply an Act of Parliament, subject to change by Parliament. As an integral part of the Constitution, the new Charter of Rights can be amended only through the elaborate procedure required for constitutional amendments. The Bill of Rights of 1960, incidentally, is still in effect and occasionally applied, though it is much narrower in scope than the Charter.

The primary impetus for Canada's Charter of Rights came from Prime Minister Trudeau who was convinced of the need for it even though several provincial premiers during the early stages of negotiations on the Constitution were opposed. The original version of the Charter underwent numerous changes during these discussions and also as a result of representations from various individuals and groups. Women and natives, for example, pressed for inclusion of clauses affecting them. The Charter in fact was revised 54 times during the course of its development — a marked contrast to what later occurred with the Meech Lake Constitutional Accord.

Never have so many opportunities been afforded to the public to express their views on proposed legislation as took place concerning the Charter. A Special Joint Parliamentary Committee held 65 days of public hearings (November 6, 1980 to February 2, 1981). It heard over 100 witnesses and received over 1,200 submissions from individuals and groups before the Charter was finalized in its present form. The whole process was a remarkable demonstration of the vitality of public participation, and might well serve as a model for the present.

Despite the fact, however, that the whole process was opened to an infinite variety of interest groups, some of the provincial premiers in the end insisted that the Charter include an override clause (section 33) which allows any legislature to expressly negate the Charter in respect to a specific law. It is known as the "notwithstanding clause." It means that if Parliament or a province were to pass a law which might infringe some right protected by the Charter, they could declare in the same piece of legislation that the law will operate "notwithstanding" the fact that it may violate the Charter of Rights.

Québec made use of this override provision in 1988 — even though that province had not signed the 1982 Constitution containing the Charter. It arose in the following way.

In 1978, Québec passed Bill 101 requiring French-only signs on all business premises throughout the province. In December 1988, this Bill was declared unconstitutional by the Supreme Court of Canada under both the Québec and Canadian Charters of Rights as violating freedom of speech and expression. Within a week of that decision, the Québec legislature passed Bill 178 requiring French only on outdoor signs and limited English signs indoors. In order to prevent the new Bill being challenged in court, as the earlier one had been, Québec added an override clause stating that the Bill would operate notwithstanding possible violation of the Charter of Rights. This was not only an affront to the Supreme Court decision, but Québec was making use of the notwithstanding clause in a Constitution which it had not signed.

Apart from Québec's use of the override clause, it has so far been invoked only once. That was by Saskatchewan in 1986 in connection with legislation ordering striking dairy workers to return to their jobs.

It is unfortunate that the Canadian Charter of Rights is saddled with the override provision, but it will be difficult to remove — for the same reasons that it was included, namely, at the insistence of some premiers.

Despite the criticism leveled against the notwithstanding clause, one of Canada's noted constitutional authorities, Peter Russell of the University of Toronto, has defended the clause in that it preserves the principle of parliamentary sovereignty. It reserves to legislatures, not the judiciary, the final say as to whether a law should prevail "notwithstanding" a possible violation of the Charter. This he considers an essential aspect of democracy.[4]

COURT DECISIONS RELATING TO THE CHARTER

As already mentioned, the Charter of Rights and Freedoms has been raised as an issue in numerous cases before Canadian courts in recent years. The Charter, for example, provides that a person charged with an offence has the right to be tried within a reasonable time (section 11(b)). A case arose in Ontario in 1983 where three persons were charged with conspiracy to commit extortion. A delay of almost two years between the preliminary hearing and the trial was held by the Supreme Court of Canada to be unreasonable, and the charges were dismissed. The Court suggested as a guideline that a delay beyond eight months for certain offences is unreasonable (*Askov*, [1990] 2 S.C.R. 1199). As a result of that ruling, numerous charges have been dismissed by courts throughout Canada, particularly in Ontario. In June 1991, a cocaine and marijuana conspiracy charge against three accused was dismissed by the Alberta Court of Queen's Bench (Matheson J.) on the same ground.

An interesting case arose in B.C. where a person was denied admission as a practising lawyer because he was not a Canadian citizen, though otherwise fully qualified. The Supreme Court of Canada held that the requirement of Canadian citizenship violated the Charter guarantee of "equality before and under the law" and the "right to equal protection and equal benefit of the law without discrimination" (section 15(1)). (Re *Andrews*, [1989] 1 S.C.R. 143).

Another application of the Charter arose in the *Big M Drug Mart* case where a Calgary store was charged with unlawfully carrying on business on Sunday contrary to the Lord's Day Act. The Supreme Court of Canada held that since the effect of the Act was to compel the observance, even by non-Christians, of the Christian sabbath, it was unconstitutional as violating the Charter's guarantee of "freedom of Conscience and Religion" (section 2(a)). The charge was accordingly dismissed ([1985] 1 S.C.R. 295).

---

[4] See: "Standing up for Notwithstanding" by Peter Russell (1991) 29 Alberta Law Review 293.

In July 1990, a native woman, convicted of murder in Saskatchewan, was given a mandatory life sentence. Madam Justice Marion Wedge of the Court of Queen's Bench, in passing sentence, stated that transferring her to the only federal women's penitentiary in Kingston, Ontario, far removed from children and friends, was "cruel and unusual punishment" contrary to section 12 of the Charter, as well as "discrimination" under section 15(1). Male prisoners have a choice of several federal penitentiaries, making their placement possible nearer to home. The Saskatchewan Court of Appeal however, overturned this finding in June 1991 on the ground that only the Federal Court of Canada could make such a declaration. A class action lawsuit, on behalf of several inmates in the Prison for Women, seeking a similar ruling, is now before the Federal Court of Canada.

A very recent decision of the Supreme Court of Canada was delivered on June 6, 1991 (the *Millar* case). It declared unconstitutional a section in the Public Service Employment Act prohibiting federal civil servants from engaging in political activities in support of a political party or candidate. This prohibition was held to be a violation of the Charter protection of "freedom of expression" (section 2(B)). This decision will enable Canada to have a permanent civil service without curtailing the political rights of its members — other than those at the senior level of policy planning.

These examples illustrate the broad grounds on which laws and procedures can be challenged under the Charter. One's viewpoint as to the Charter depends on how important we consider the matter of individual protection in contemporary society. Obviously the drafters of the Charter considered individual rights to be of paramount importance. So also have the courts in the many cases coming before them requiring a judicial interpretation of the meaning and spirit of the Charter.

Herein lies a fundamental difference in philosophy between French and English Canada. On certain issues, the Québec government attaches less importance to individual rights than to what they call "collective" rights. This manifests itself in the following way: Promotion of the French language, as a *collective* policy for the advancement of French, is more important to the government of Québec than any infringement this may cause to the *individual* rights of the English-speaking minority. Québec had ignored English language rights when it enacted Bill 178 prohibiting English outdoor signs. In other words the collective value of promoting French was allowed to take precedence over the rights of individuals affected by the law. The same thing arose with the Meech Lake Accord, when Québec opposed the addition of a single clause which would make the "distinct society" clause subject to the Charter, so that collective rights would be secondary to individual rights.

The Charter does contain a "balancing" provision (section 1) which can prevent a law being declared invalid. Even though a law or action is found to violate a right guaranteed by the Charter, the courts need not declare it invalid if it is a "reasonable limit" on rights such as would be "justified in a free and democratic society." This exemption does give some scope for flexibility from the strict enforcement of the Charter provisions.

There have been literally hundreds of court cases where section 1 has been raised in an attempt to preserve a law or practice which would otherwise be in violation of the Charter. One of the leading cases is Regina v. Oakes (19 Cdn. Rights Reporter 308), a decision of the Supreme Court of Canada in 1986. Section 8 of the Narcotics Control Act provides that if a court finds an accused in possession of a narcotic, he is presumed to be in possession for the purpose of trafficking, and unless he can produce evidence to the contrary, he will be convicted of the more serious crime of trafficking. The Court held that this section violates the presumption of innocence guaranteed in section 11(d) of the Charter. It was argued that since section 8 was aimed at curbing drug trafficking by facilitating the conviction of drug traffickers, it was a "reasonable limit" to be placed on the Charter protection. However, Chief Justice Brian Dickson held that the Charter must prevail since the presumption of innocence is "a hallowed principle lying at the very heart of the criminal law."

When we speak of Canada's Constitution, we mean:
- the BNA Act 1867, which is our basic Constitution;
- the Statute of Westminster 1931, giving Canada full power over foreign affairs;
- the Canada Act 1982, transferring Canada's Constitution from Britain to Canada;
- the Constitution Act 1982, with a new amending formula, recognition of aboriginal rights, equality of economic opportunities and the right to public services;
- the Charter of Rights and Freedoms 1982 protecting citizens from abuses by the state.

Another case in the Supreme Court in 1988 led to the opposite result: *Hufsky v. A.G. of Canada* (32 Cdn. Rights Reporter 193). There, an accused was charged with refusing to provide a roadside breath simple as required by the Criminal Code (section 234.1(1)). The accused said this infringed his right under the Charter not to be arbitrarily detained (section 9). The Court upheld the requirement for the breath sample as a "reasonable limit" on the accused's rights because of the serious consequences of impaired driving and the difficulty of detecting violations except through random road tests.

Whatever we may think of the wisdom or otherwise of Canada's constitutional Charter of Rights, it is and will remain a very significant aspect of our Constitution. As such, it is in keeping with the constitutions of most other Western countries.

4 THE MEECH LAKE CONSTITUTIONAL ACCORD

POLITICAL BACKGROUND

It will be seen that the Liberal Party has been in power for most of the past 50 years (until 1984). This is because the Liberals have traditionally won most of the Québec seats in the House of Commons. It has long been assumed that the party that controls Québec is assured of a federal victory: Québec now has an allotment of 79 seats out of the total of 295 seats in the House of Commons. Stated differently, no party can remain in power without a strong political base in Québec.

In the federal election of 1980, the Conservatives under Joe Clark gained just one seat in Québec. In the 1984 election, Mr. Mulroney won 58 Québec seats by appealing to Québec nationalists (even separatists) through a promise of a "better deal" for Québec within the Canadian Constitution. To this day, he remains dependent on this group for support in order to remain in power. Mr. Mulroney arrived in Ottawa in 1984 with a strong contingent of Québec Conservatives, some of them former separatists, many having little or no experience in federal politics and with little affection for Canadian federalism. However, Mr. Mulroney believed that the constitutional changes which he had promised would convert the Québec sceptics in his government from their nationalistic ambitions. This has clearly not happened — as seen by the defection of such key Ministers as Lucien Bouchard in 1990, and his formation of the Bloc Québécois in the House of Commons.

The following is a list of Prime Ministers from 1935 to the present:

- Mackenzie King
  1935 — 1948   (L)
- St. Laurent
  1948 — 1957   (L)
- John Diefenbaker
  1957 — 1963   (PC)
- Lester Pearson
  1963 — 1968   (L)
- Pierre Trudeau
  1968 — 1979
  1980 — 1984   (L)
- Joe Clark
  1979 (9 months)   (PC)
- John Turner
  1984 (3 months)   (L)
- Brian Mulroney
  1984 — present   (PC)

At the present time, of the 159 Conservative MPs in the House of Commons, 57 are from Québec. Thus, it is obvious how important it is for Mr. Mulroney to retain the loyalty of his Québec caucus.

Throughout the ongoing constitutional negotiations it is important for Canadians to understand the political factors involved and the reason for the Prime Minister's preoccupation with Québec's demands. Simply put, most people believe that at the time of the 1984 election he made a "marriage of political convenience" with separatists in Québec and he is still beholden to them.

Not long after Mr. Mulroney came to power, he began negotiations with Québec to fulfil his promise to bring that province into the Constitution "with honour, enthusiasm and dignity." These negotiations led eventually to the Meech Lake Constitutional Accord.

HOW THE ACCORD BEGAN AND ENDED

The goal of the Meech Lake Accord was a perfectly laudable one — to obtain Québec's endorsement to the Constitution Act of 1982, from which Québec had excluded itself. When proposed by Prime Minister Mulroney in 1987, the Meech Lake Accord was intended as another amendment to the Constitution. Its purpose was to respond to five demands presented by Québec as the condition for it signing the Constitution.

The Prime Minister summoned the ten provincial premiers for two meetings — the first at Meech Lake (April 30, 1987), the second in Ottawa (June 3, 1987). They met in secret. They emerged with a final document which was to be ratified by Parliament and the ten provincial legislatures within three years. The Premiers at the time were:

Bill Vander Zalm (PC) B.C.; Don Getty (PC) Alberta; Grant Devine (PC) Saskatchewan; Howard Pawley (NDP) Manitoba; David Peterson (L) Ontario; Robert Bourassa (L) Québec; John Buchanan (PC) Nova Scotia; Richard Hatfield (PC) New Brunswick; Joe Ghiz (L) P.E.I.; Brian Peckford (PC) Newfoundland.

As of June, 1991, only four of the original ten remained in office, the following having been replaced: Peckford, Hatfield, Buchanan, Peterson, Pawley, Vander Zalm; and another (Devine) facing an early uncertain election.

The Accord was readily ratified by Parliament and initially by eight of the ten provinces. However, elections took place which brought about a change of government in three provinces, with three new premiers namely:

• *Frank McKenna* (L) in New Brunswick replacing Premier Hatfield (PC), McKenna gaining all the seats in the Legislature (October 1987);

• *Gary Filmon* (PC) in Manitoba heading a minority government replacing the NDP government of Howard Pawley — April 1988. This election gave Sharon Carstairs, the Liberal Opposition leader the balance of power in the Manitoba Legislature, and a very influential role in the debate over the Meech Lake Accord;

• *Clyde Wells* (L) of Newfoundland replacing Brian Peckford (PC) on April 20, 1989. The Newfoundland House of Assembly on April 6, 1990 revoked the earlier Peckford government's ratification of the Meech Lake Accord.[5]

Each of these new Premiers vehemently opposed the Meech Lake Accord. Premier McKenna was the first to voice his opposition and he continued to do so with effectiveness and sincerity, though eventually he capitulated. This was not before he had made a valiant effort to introduce amendments, but failed. The Accord, however, was never approved by Manitoba and Newfoundland. The Prime Minister has persisted in the myth of blaming its defeat on Newfoundland Premier Clyde Wells. This represents a distortion of the facts, as shown by the following chronology of events.

The Meech Lake Accord died in the Manitoba Legislature hours before it was to be taken to a vote in the Newfoundland House of Assembly. It died in Manitoba because a native MLA named Elijah Harper Jr. refused to give the unanimous approval necessary under Manitoba law for dispensing with public hearings before having a vote on the Accord. It died when this Ojibway Cree Indian, representing the constituency of Red Sucker Lake in northern Manitoba, held

---

5 It is interesting to note how quickly political personalities can change, thus casting doubt on the significance of agreements reached by First Ministers — the Prime Minister and ten premiers (Executive Federalism). A striking illustration of this is how the key players in the 1982 Constitution have largely disappeared. There were ten premiers, one Prime Minister and nine justices of the Supreme Court involved in that constitution (20 in all). Of these, only one remains, namely Mr. Justice Lamer, now Chief Justice of the Supreme Court of Canada. All of the other 19 have disappeared from public life — all within a decade.

an eagle feather in his right hand at 12:24 p.m. (noon) on Friday June 22, 1990 and said a single quiet word — "NO." This happened even though at the eleventh hour the Prime Minister had offered to set up a royal commission on aboriginal affairs in the hope of gaining native approval to the Accord.

The events in the Manitoba legislature led Premier Wells to rightly conclude there was no purpose in having his legislature vote on the Accord since its rejection in Manitoba had ended any possibility of the Accord achieving the necessary unanimity.

Mr. Mulroney, in his anger, however, deemed it more expedient politically to blame Clyde Wells rather than a native Indian from Manitoba for what was really his own personal failure. Of all the premiers involved in the Meech Lake debate, Premier Wells was undoubtedly the leading expert on constitutional law. Mr. Mulroney had long resented his astute analysis of flaws in the Accord, which Mr. Wells had expressed in his first encounter with the Prime Minister at the First Ministers' Conference in November 1989. However, throughout this whole period, it was Mr. Wells who spoke out strongly for Canada, while some of the other premiers seemed more concerned about promoting their own political interests.

Special reference should be made here to Sharon Carstairs. As Liberal opposition leader in Manitoba, her party held the balance of power in the minority government of Premier Gary Filmon following the Manitoba election in April 1988. Mr. Filmon originally favoured the Accord and planned to introduce a resolution in the Manitoba legislature to ratify it. However, Sharon Carstairs, having expressed strong opposition to the Accord, made it clear that her party would bring down the government if he attempted to do so. Her brilliant, non-partisan and responsible objections expressed not only in the Manitoba legislature, but through interviews with press, radio and television served to enlighten many Canadians as to the implications of the Accord. After Premier Filmon changed his position in December 1988 (largely because of Québec's passage of Bill 178), he became one of the strongest leaders opposing the Accord. Manitoba's objection was based on the most complete public hearings held in any province, during which a committee visited many communities and heard over 300 presentations, most of them opposed to the Accord. Five provinces held no formal public hearings at all. Premier Filmon, to his credit, continued to work closely with both his opposition leaders, even inviting them to accompany him to Ottawa as consultants at the final meeting of First Ministers in June.

It should be pointed out, however, that the Meech Lake Accord failed for other reasons than the objection of certain premiers. It failed because the people of Canada did not want it, and their voices had not been heeded. Canadians opposed the Accord for two reasons: both for what it said, and for how it was created; in other words, both because of its content and because of the process which attempted to force its adoption. These aspects will be examined now.

ITS CONTENTS

Québec had five original demands as conditions of its acceptance of the 1982 Constitution Act:

◆ recognition of Québec as a "distinct society;"

◆ increased powers for Québec over immigration;

◆ a role for Québec in the appointment of Supreme Court judges;

removal of any restrictions over how federal money is spent by Québec in shared-cost programs (such as education, health and welfare) including the right to opt-out and receive compensation;

◆ the right of Québec to a veto over all future constitutional changes.

The Meech Lake Accord would have granted all of Québec's demands and in addition would have added two more not included in Québec's original proposals, namely:

◆ the right of provincial governments to nominate Senators, the final selection remaining with the federal government;

◆ annual constitutional conferences of the Prime Minister and provincial Premiers (which might have led to more closed sessions of the Meech Lake type).

In order to get the approval of the other nine premiers to the concessions being granted to Québec, Mr. Mulroney offered similar powers to all the provinces, thus weakening the central government in its role as the nation's unifying force. It would have meant a transfer of powers away from the federal government at a time when Canada needed (and still needs) strength at its centre, an authority to speak for all Canadians, to arbitrate on national issues, to overcome regional disparities and to fulfil a leadership role in respect to social, economic and environmental concerns. Though Québec had legitimate demands that needed to be addressed, the real fault lay in the attitude of the other nine premiers who so readily accepted powers that rightly belong to the central government. It was their attitude, even more so than Québec's, which deserves criticism.

The Accord would have given Québec the power to "preserve and promote" its "distinct society." It failed to take into account the interests of natives, women, minorities and northerners. It preserved the English-French duality of Canada. It gave to every province a veto over major constitutional changes, so that any one province could block amendments in future.[6]

EFFORTS AT ACHIEVING ACCEPTANCE

The general strategy

The basic complaint about the Meech Lake Accord was the undemocratic manner in which it was handled. It was forged in secret in 1987 at a meeting of 11 men whose election mandates had not included authority to make sweeping (and binding) constitutional changes. Even though Canadians had no part in its preparation, it was nonetheless presented to the public as a final unalterable constitutional document, not subject to amendment. For that reason, a national debate (had there been one) would have been meaningless. Throughout the three-year period allowed for its ratification, serious impasses developed, yet Québec remained adamant to the end in refusing to allow any changes, and the Mulroney government allied itself to the Québec position.

The general strategy, instead of attempting to justify the Accord on its merits, was to use threats, warnings and ultimatums as to what would happen if it were rejected. Intense efforts were made to coerce the three dissenting premiers (McKenna, Filmon and Wells) to accept the Accord by discrediting them, isolating and manipulating them, and blaming them for destroying Canada if it failed.

---

[6] Full details of the Accord are contained in the author's national best-selling book entitled "The Meech Lake Accord: What it will mean to you and to Canada," Voyageur Press 1990.

It was becoming apparent to Canadians that the side-effects of the Accord if adopted could be as detrimental to national unity as its rejection. Québec could use the Accord as an open door to independence simply by utilizing to the limit the "distinct society" clause. It could eventually claim that the only way to achieve its distinct society would be by becoming independent. In other words, rejection or acceptance of the Accord could be used by Québec as a pretext to leave Canada, if it chose.

Premier McKenna's proposal

It was not until early 1990 (over two years after the Accord had been signed in 1987 and six months before the deadline for ratification) that the issue was thrust into the national headlines. The three dissenting premiers (all newly elected since 1987) had made it clear that they would not accept the Accord without changes.

Just when the situation appeared hopeless, Premier Frank McKenna of New Brunswick (one of the three dissenting premiers) presented a proposal on March 21, 1990 for a so-called "Parallel Accord." It would deal with unresolved issues, such as rights of women, natives, minorities, northern Canadians, Senate reform, clarification of the distinct society clause and the unanimity requirement for amendments. If approved, it could be signed at the same time, as a kind of "Companion Accord."

Appointment of a Special Parliamentary Committee

Prime Minister Mulroney welcomed the New Brunswick proposal, and tabled a resolution in the House of Commons on March 26 (over the objections of Québec) under which a Special Parliamentary Committee (all party) would be established to consider a Parallel Accord and to conduct public hearings. This Committee (later to be known as the "Charest Committee" after its Chairman, Jean Charest of Québec) consisted of 15 MPs (nine Tories including four from Québec, four Liberals, two NDP).

During the course of the next three weeks, the committee held hearings throughout the country, albeit (because of time constraints) in only six cities (Ottawa, Yellowknife, Whitehorse, Vancouver,

Winnipeg and St. John's, Newfoundland). It heard 160 witnesses and received 800 written submissions. Yet even before the hearings commenced, the Québec National Assembly on April 15 passed a Resolution rejecting any changes to the Accord. A national poll taken in early May 1990 showed that 69 per cent of Canadians were opposed to the Accord in its present form.

The Committee invited written submissions, from which it selected persons for oral presentations. All the proceedings were covered on national television.

The Charest Report

On May 17, after three weeks of hearings, the Committee released its report (now called the "Charest Report"), containing 23 recommendations. It was unanimous, which is remarkable, considering that its members were from all three political parties.

The report recommended that the Meech Lake Accord be signed by June 23, provided there was sufficient certainty that additional reforms would follow through a Companion Accord. But, many people believed that the suggested changes were too important to be relegated to a Companion Accord. Others expressed the view that if the Accord necessitated 23 recommendations, it must be seriously flawed in the first place. Whatever its deficiencies, however, the Charest Report offered the one hope at that late date for achieving a compromise solution to the Meech Lake Accord.

The reaction of Québec was an immediate and angry rejection of the Report. Premier Bourassa made it clear that his government would refuse to discuss changes until after the Accord was signed. Once signed, of course, the Accord would give Québec a veto over any major future amendments. Release of the Report also led to the immediate resignation of Environmental Minister Lucien Bouchard, the leading federal Cabinet Minister from Québec and close friend of Brian Mulroney. He would later form the Bloc Québécois, a separatist group of MPs in the House of Commons.

Because of Québec's reaction, the Prime Minister gave no further consideration to the Charest Report even though it represented the unanimous views of an all-party Committee and was based on the only federal public hearings during the three year debate on the Meech Lake Accord.[7]

Subsequent efforts by the Prime Minister

With rejection of the Charest Report by the Prime Minister, the Meech Lake Accord reverted to its former impasse. Only 37 days remained from the tabling of that Report until the June 23 deadline. It seemed imperative (and the Charest Report recommended) that no time be lost in convening a meeting of the provincial premiers since only they at that stage could possibly negotiate a solution. However, the Prime Minister delayed calling such a meeting for some 17 days (until June 3), all the while purporting to confer with the Premiers on an individual basis. He would later admit during an interview in *The Globe & Mail* (June 20, 1990) that this was part of his preconceived plan to create a crisis atmosphere in the hope that under the pressure of the approaching deadline, the three dissenting premiers would capitulate. He called it "rolling the dice."

During late May, the Prime Minister resorted to a series of tactics: he sent his special envoy, Senator Lowell Murray, who was not an elected official, across the country to talk to the premiers, then he met with them individually on a one-to-one basis at his residence in Ottawa. Canadians were not informed as to what was being discussed at these meetings or what powers might be bargained away. A final attempt was made on May 29 when Senator Murray was again sent to Newfoundland for further talks with Premier Wells, who along with Premier Filmon of Manitoba, continued adamant in their refusal to accept the Meech Lake Accord without substantial changes.

Finally, with only three weeks remaining before the June 23 deadline, the Prime Minister invited the premiers to dinner in Ottawa on June 3 — a dinner that would lead to the longest meeting of First Ministers ever held.

---

[7] For clarification, it can be mentioned that in July 1987, as the Resolution approving of the Meech Lake Accord was passing through Parliament, hearings were held in Ottawa following second reading of the Bill. There were 249 briefs received and 80 witnesses heard, many of them opposed to the Accord even then. However, Prime Minister Mulroney announced in advance that he would not be influenced by the results of those hearings. The Accord was accordingly passed by Parliament. Hearings of this kind on second reading of a Bill are normal parliamentary procedure but in no way are they a substitute for the kind of national debate that should have taken place on the Accord.

The Ottawa Conference (June 3-9 inclusive)

For seven days the Prime Minister and ten provincial premiers met in isolation and secrecy on the fifth floor of the Conference Centre in Ottawa. They rejected a proposal from Premiers Filmon and Wells that the session be open to television coverage. The only information released to the public throughout the week consisted of snatches of interviews with the politicians which the media caught for the nightly television news.

The secrecy which marked the entire proceedings from beginning to end was in sharp contrast to the procedure followed during the 1982 Constitution negotiations, in which Canadians from all walks of life were given abundant opportunities to offer insights, suggestions and opinions as to what their Constitution should contain — many being incorporated into the ongoing revisions.

Canadians never did learn details of the heated and bitter arguments that went on during the 77 hours of secret meetings in Ottawa, but we do know that Premiers Filmon and Wells were subjected to tremendous pressure to capitulate. Premier Frank McKenna, encouraged by the possibility of future amendments, eventually acquiesced, even though he could not get the changes he once thought necessary. However, he will be long remembered as the first premier to raise doubts about the Accord back in 1987, and who, by his proposal in 1990 for a Companion Accord, provided the only meaningful attempt to break the deadlock, even though his efforts failed.

An attempt was made to add a "Canada clause" to provide a balance to the distinct society clause. It would have recognized "the fundamental characteristics of Canada" such as multiculturalism, native rights, official languages — but it met with objections from Québec.

Many times during the seven day session, the talks seemed on the verge of collapse. It was a period of emotional ups and downs, not only for the 11 premiers, but for the general public as well. Finally, on Saturday evening (June 9), the First Ministers emerged from seclusion to appear on national television in an apparent jubilant mood. Moments before, Premier Wells had been angered to discover that a key clause on which he had insisted (regarding the relation between the Charter and the distinct society clause) had been omitted — once more at the insistence of Québec, to which the Prime Minister acquiesced by deleting the clause, but without informing Premier Wells.

The final communique confirmed that the Meech Lake Accord would remain unchanged. No Companion Accord was attached. Instead, a "First Ministers' Agreement" was appended, listing items for action after (but only after) the Accord was ratified (which would give a veto to all provinces). The proposals for future consideration included: Senate reform, language rights, sexual equality, aboriginal concerns, territorial rights, the creation of new provinces. The fact that the Meech Lake Accord required such extensive additions as these raises considerable doubt about its worth as a constitutional document. Appended to the Agreement as well was a legal opinion of "six legal specialists" containing an interpretation of the distinct society clause in relation to the Charter. The opinion, which declared the Charter to be unaffected by the Accord, was greeted with considerable scepticism by legal scholars. Indeed, there were parallel legal opinions which reached the opposite conclusion. The Dean of Law at Queen's University, John D. Whyte (writing in *The Globe and Mail*, June 15, 1990) described the letter as "confusing in intent, substance and effect."

This then was the communique signed by the Prime Minister and ten provincial premiers before the television cameras, marking the culmination of seven days of secret deliberations. When each individually gave his emotional closing speech, it was Newfoundland Premier Wells who spoke with deepest sincerity for Canada. He had already won the acclaim of citizens throughout the country, evidenced by the flood of mail, telegrams and phone calls that reached his office during the final weeks of the debate. In signing the communique he made it clear that he would take it back to his people in Newfoundland for either a referendum, or for a free vote in his legislature on June 22. Premier Filmon promised to comply with Manitoba law which required a debate in the Legislature and public hearings before a vote on the Accord could be taken. Mr. Filmon had long before advised the Prime Minister that this procedure would take a minimum of three weeks. Yet he had been left with only 12 days.

Of all the premiers, only Filmon and Wells followed the democratic procedure of consulting their electorates. When Premier Wells returned to Newfoundland there was not sufficient time for a referendum; so he sent all the Members to their home ridings to get the views of their constituents before the scheduled vote on June 22. Likewise,

Premier Filmon adhered to the strict parliamentary procedure required by Manitoba law. Nothing approaching this democratic process was followed by any of the six premiers whose legislatures had readily ratified the Accord some two years before.

It should be mentioned that for all his intransigence, Premier Robert Bourassa performed with dignity at the Ottawa meetings, assuming at times even a conciliatory attitude. But he was subjected to extreme pressure from his opposition back home, which forced him to maintain an unbending position. Understandably, Mr. Mulroney, dependent on Québec for his political survival, consistently supported Québec in its stand, but in so doing seriously compromised his responsibility as the prime advocate for all Canada.

The final days and the Accord's collapse

The euphoria of June 9 proved to be a fleeting triumph.

It soon became evident that there was insufficient time for the Accord to be ratified under the democratic procedure required in Manitoba and Newfoundland. For three years the Prime Minister had insisted that the June 23 deadline was fixed and firm. Then, in a panic on June 22, he said it might be extended, and if Premier Wells would only ratify the Accord, the Prime Minister would seek a reference to the Supreme Court of Canada on the legality of a possible extension — something which he had consistently refused to do when earlier requested. The purpose of such an extension (the Prime Minister said) would be to give Manitoba more time. It seemed that if Manitoba were to be granted more time, so also should Newfoundland. Wells would later refer to this as a cynical last-minute strategy — in his words "the final manipulation." It would later be revealed that the scheme of extending the deadline as a last-minute ploy had been conceived a year earlier.

Likewise, at the eleventh hour, in an attempt to get Manitoba's approval, Mr. Mulroney sent a delegation to Winnipeg with a six-page letter, promising Elijah Harper Jr. he would set up a Royal Commission on Native Affairs provided Harper would withdraw his objection. Yet for three years the Canadian Human Rights Commission had been requesting the federal government to establish such a Commission. Despite this and other requests, nothing was done until May 1991, almost a year later.

In the end, the Meech Lake Accord failed the democratic test and died without ratification. Thus ended Canada's agonizing saga of manipulation, deception and coercion — against which in the end the principles of democracy ultimately prevailed.

LESSONS FROM MEECH LAKE

1. The collapse of the Meech Lake Accord marks the end of Executive Federalism as a tool of government. This is the system whereby decisions are finalized by First Ministers (the Prime Minister and provincial Premiers). In future, the democratic process will be expected to take precedence.

2. Canada's Constitution belongs to the people and not to politicians.

3. Constitutional change cannot be based on the demands of one province. It must be balanced and equitable for all Canadians.

4. The public is far more intelligent than politicians are inclined to believe. Canadians were quick to detect deception and manipulation. They interpreted the Prime Minister's "rolling the dice" as gambling with the country's future.

5. When the polls clearly showed that the majority of the electorate did not approve of what the politicians were doing, the error was in not giving people a chance to be heard, or alternatively having the government seek a new mandate.

6. The supreme error was in presenting this as a constitutional document which could not be altered, and adhering to that position throughout the entire three-year period allowed for its ratification.

7. It was improper for politicians and the media to present the Accord simply as a conflict between English and French, or between Québec and the rest of Canada — when there were many other grounds for objection to the Accord. By improperly focusing on these narrow issues, national tension was exacerbated.

8. The truth (not sufficiently stressed) was that English Canada was not rejecting Québec; it was rejecting the dismantling of federalism. It was not saying NO to Québec, but NO to a fragmented country.

9. Presenting the issues in a false light was bound to foment discord. The initial purpose of Meech Lake was simply to obtain the signature of Québec to the 1982 Constitution. Yet it was allowed to explode into a national crisis of major proportions — thereby assuming a status that was never intended and should never have been allowed. One would almost assume there was some political motivation to this distortion. Some have suggested that the Prime Minister was anxious to make this his one great achievement to match that of the former Prime Minister who had finalized the earlier Constitution.

10. The reality was that the Meech Lake Accord, if adopted, would not have satisfied Québec's expectations. Yet its collapse was bound to intensify the movement towards sovereignty.

11. History will show that the two dissenting premiers, by following democratic procedure, spared Canada from having a constitution imposed against the will of a majority of Canadians, whose lingering rancour and resentment would have been damaging to Canada.

12. Finally, constitutional changes will never be achieved by arbitrary decisions, but only through a slow, deliberative and rational process, within a more flexible time frame, and in an atmosphere of reason, cooperation, good-will and respect amongst leaders who must themselves be prepared to submerge self-interests for the national good. This is an essential, though not unreasonable, prerequisite for the success of any future constitutional talks.

5

THE AFTERMATH OF THE MEECH LAKE ACCORD

WHAT IF MEECH LAKE HAD PASSED?

1. It would have angered a large number of Canadians who were opposed to it. (Polls at the time showed 59 per cent of Canadians did not approve of the Accord.)

2. Even if it had been ratified, it would not have satisfied Québec's demands or expectations.

3. It would have entrenched the French/English version of Canada which no longer represents the demographic reality.

4. The Canadian federation would have had unequal provinces with Québec having the greater powers. Alternatively, if all provinces were given similar powers, the cohesiveness of the federation would have been undermined.

5. Too little power would have been left to the federal government to do the things that a federal government should do.

6. Senate appointments would have become a form of provincial patronage which would have been no improvement over the existing complaints of patronage.

7. The unanimity rule for constitutional amendments would have frustrated advocates of Senate reform.

8. Allowing judges of the Supreme Court of Canada to be nominated by the provinces could have politicized the process and compromised the judicial independence of Canada's highest court.

9. Immigration powers given to the provinces (such as Québec demanded for itself) would have resulted in competition for immigrants, whose allegiance to the nation would have been weakened through provincial control over their orientation.

10. Provinces would have had the right to opt-out of shared-cost programs, putting an end to uniform national standards.

11. Provincial status for the Territories could have been indefinitely delayed because of the need for unanimous approval of Parliament and all provinces.

12. Québec's promotion of its distinct society could have led to repression of minorities, as was already done in Bill 178 prohibiting English outdoor signs.

13. The Accord could have been the slow road to separation, if independence were perceived by Québec as its only way to achieve its distinct society.

14. The rigid amending formula over major constitutional changes could have resulted in constitutional paralysis.

REACTIONS TO THE ACCORD'S COLLAPSE

Ottawa's reaction

The collapse of the Meech Lake Accord was a devastating blow to the federal government and to the politicians who supported it. With no contingency plan in place (which would have been the mark of good statesmanship), the Prime Minister drifted indecisively. His immediate response was to give his full attention to Québec with an eye to preserving his political base there, with little sensitivity being shown to the rest of the country. Whatever plans he may have had for resurrecting the constitutional debate were at best vague. His standing at the polls as at June 27, 1990, following the collapse of the Accord, fell to the lowest of any Prime Minister since opinion polls were first recorded a half century ago. His earlier predictions of financial disaster if the Accord was not ratified proved unfounded: the stock and bond markets remained healthy and the Canadian dollar within days hit an 11-year high. The government had then to reassure international investors that it was still safe to invest in Canada, despite its earlier warnings to the contrary.

As a demonstration of the political paralysis at the federal level, no concrete proposals for renewal of constitutional talks were forthcoming from June until November, when the Spicer Commission was appointed.

Québec's reaction

Premier Bourassa's immediate reaction took three forms:
- refusal to participate in any future constitutional talks with the provinces;

- insistence on dealing only with Ottawa on a bilateral basis;

- the taking of immediate steps to redefine Québec's relationship with Canada.

Certainly the failure of the Accord inflamed Québec nationalism. Canada's alleged rejection of Québec soon turned into Québec's rejection of Canada.

The reaction of provincial premiers

The inability of the federal government to come forward with an alternative plan led to the provincial premiers demanding more powers for themselves. The annual Premiers' Conference held in Winnipeg in August 1990 was the first without Québec. The majority of the premiers were described in the press as being "regionally-minded." However, Premier David Peterson of Ontario aptly warned: "We must not conduct ourselves like warlords trying to divide up a dying kingdom." Over the next several months, most provincial governments announced plans for establishing their own commissions on constitutional reform.

Thus, for the months following the collapse of Meech Lake, the general impression was of a country whose Prime Minister was concerned primarily with Québec, nine provincial premiers concerned mostly with themselves, and Québec sensing little affinity for either.

Public reaction

The general mood throughout Canada during the summer of 1990 fluctuated between anger and despair, disillusionment and frustration — not because Meech Lake had failed, but because of the falsehood and manipulation that accompanied it.

As one reporter said, Meech is not dead but will live for years to come as the moment when Canadians lost faith in the system which excluded them. Many thought the country should take an extended break from discussing constitutional issues. As Canadians were becoming increasingly uneasy about the future, they yearned for decisive leadership at the national level.

It was evident throughout Canada that time was needed to rebuild trust and overcome the deepening sense of public cynicism.

Native reaction

Native people were incensed that a fundamental change in the Constitution would have excluded them altogether from the process.

It was not a long leap from the Meech Lake fiasco to the Oka crisis which arose during the summer of 1990, within weeks of the collapse of the Accord. That event was more than a quarrel over a piece of land which the Mohawks claimed was theirs. It was a manifestation of wider native discontent, inflamed by disregard for their interests in the constitutional scheme.

The Meech Lake Accord had set off a chain reaction amongst native peoples. While Québec was making demands for some form of sovereignty, a minority within Québec's own borders was demanding sovereignty for itself. The Mohawk stance against Québec was really a mirror image of what Québec was demanding from Ottawa. Yet the Québec government said it would never accede to native demands. In the end, when Québec had to call on the Canadian government to send in troops to restore order, its dependence on Canada became glaringly apparent.

In essence, the reaction of natives to the Meech Lake affair was an acceleration of their demands for recognition. This would manifest itself during the months ahead by further episodes across Canada in the form of standoffs, road blockades and even violent encounters. The Meech Lake affair had set off a disintegrative force — Québec against Canada, natives against Québec.

6

MOOD IN QUÉBEC FOLLOWING
FAILURE OF MEECH LAKE

The Québec government lost no time in venting its anger at the repudiation by Canada of its basic demands. A new wave of nationalism swept through the province. Within five days of the demise of the Meech Lake Accord, Premier Bourassa set up a Special Commission on the Constitution (later to be known as the Belanger-Campeau Commission) to define Québec's political future. An earlier Committee under Jean Allaire, established by the Québec Liberal party in February 1990, changed its mandate to designing a plan for a new independent Québec. These two bodies would be working simultaneously but independently over the next six months to redefine Québec's relationship with Canada.

BILATERAL AGREEMENTS WITH OTTAWA

Québec began immediately to negotiate with Ottawa an immigration agreement giving to Québec the powers it would have received under the Meech Lake Accord. Immigration under the Constitution (1867, section 95) is a field of shared jurisdiction between the federal and provincial governments.

The bilateral agreement which was finalized on December 21, 1990 guarantees to Québec a fixed share (25 per cent) of all immigrants entering Canada each year, as well as the right to select them. Québec will provide language and cultural integration services (formerly the role of the federal government), for which the province will be compensated $332 million over five years.

Other provinces are negotiating agreements with Ottawa over immigration, but none as sweeping and far-reaching as that finalized with Québec. Each province is to supply lists of occupations in short supply and the number of immigrants needed. To that extent, immigrants can be selected on the basis of job skills and labour shortages.

Québec has also requested bilateral agreements with Ottawa over such areas as manpower training, telecommunications, unemployment insurance, and certain national programs.

However, objections are being voiced by several provincial premiers concerning bilateral deals of this nature which could amount to amending the Constitution without consent of Parliament and the provinces. Such agreements may not be in the interests of the country as a whole, and could have a decentralizing effect. With Canada in the process of redefining itself, this is not the time to bargain away powers in piecemeal fashion. In future negotiations, such powers (if not already forfeited) might be crucial enough to induce Québec to remain in Canada.

THE ALLAIRE REPORT

This derives its name from its chairman, Jean Allaire, a Montréal lawyer and member of the Québec National Assembly. He headed a committee appointed by Premier Bourassa to prepare a plan for Québec's future, for use by the Québec Liberal party, in the light of the failure of the Meech Lake Accord.

Its 60-page report entitled "A Québec Free to Choose" was released on January 30, 1991. It called for a radical shift in powers from Ottawa under the threat of separation. This transfer of powers would include 22 fields now shared with, or exclusively controlled by, the federal government. The shared powers to be transferred to Québec would include control over manpower, tourism, agriculture, communications, regional development, energy, environment, research and development, public security. The powers now exclusively federal which would be transferred to Québec include foreign policy, transport, fisheries, postal service, native affairs; leaving to the federal government control over the following only: defence, customs and tariffs (meaningless with U.S. free trade), currency, the national debt, and equalization payments from Ottawa to the provinces (including presumably payments to Québec). In other words, this Report would emasculate the central government, rendering it so enfeebled as to be unable to govern effectively. Indeed, it would virtually dismantle the federal system of Canada.

The Report contains other recommendations, namely: that the Senate be abolished; that the Canadian Charter of Rights and Freedoms not apply to Québec; that Québec adopt a new Constitution with its own Supreme Court, as the final Court of Appeal in civil matters; that an amending formula in Canada's existing Constitution give Québec a veto over all constitutional changes. The Canadian Parliament, despite its narrow powers, would still have Québec MPs; that is, Québec would have a say in how Canada is run though Canada would have no say in how Québec is run. Unless an agreement on these terms is reached with Canada by the fall of 1992, a referendum on sovereignty would be held in Québec.

The Report was circulated for debate for five weeks amongst the Liberal riding associations and presented to the Québec Liberal Party Convention on March 9, 1991. In the end, it was endorsed with little modification as the official policy of the Bourassa Liberal Party. The only changes were that the Senate would not be abolished, but reformed; and the Canadian Charter of Rights and Freedoms would apply to Québec. Debate at the Convention was known to be sharp and acrimonious. At one point Claude Ryan, senior cabinet minister in Bourassa's government and a staunch federalist, walked out after the Convention rejected his attempt to soften the motion. He returned only when Bourassa assured him that federalism remained the Party's first choice. It is known that the Convention was dominated by a large group of radical youth delegates, for whom an independent Québec has special appeal.

Premier Bourassa was probably forced to accept a hard line in order to placate the nationalists within his own party, whose support is needed if he is to continue in power. In his closing speech he reinforced his own commitment to Canada. His later comments seemed designed to diminish the importance of the Report. He referred to it as merely an initial bargaining position for the next round of constitutional talks, and he praised it for giving Canada one more chance to negotiate. An opinion poll taken in Québec in February 1991 showed that 60 per cent of Québecers were in favour of renewed federalism, not separation. By May 1991 the figure in support of renewed federalism had risen to 71 per cent (Southam Unity Survey).

BELANGER-CAMPEAU COMMISSION

Its structure

The country had no sooner absorbed the shock of the Allaire Report when another more sweeping publication was released. This one (known as the Belanger–Campeau Report) was to become the official position of the Québec government, not simply of the Liberal Party of Québec (as in the case of the Allaire Report).

Premier Bourassa announced the creation of this Commission at the end of June, 1990, immediately after the collapse of the Meech Lake Accord, and it was officially established by the Québec National Assembly on September 4, 1990. Its official title was the "Commission on the Political and Constitutional Future of Québec." Its mandate was simple: to explore Québec's constitutional future. It was required to report by March 28, 1991.

Its Co-Chairmen were Michel Belanger, retired Chairman of the National Bank of Canada and a strong separatist; and Jean Campeau, Chairman of Domtar, a strong federalist in the 1980 Québec referendum and a former provincial deputy minister of industry and commerce. It had 36 members, several being non-politicians. Its 23 politicians came from different political parties (18 being members of the Québec National Assembly, three were Québec federal MPs, including Lucien Bouchard who had defected from the Tories, and two elected municipal officials). Its outside members included six business leaders, four trade unionists, one educator, an artist and a trade official. It is notable that the two main political leaders in Québec (Robert Bourassa of the Liberals and Jacques Parizeau of the Parti Québécois) were members.

This Commission was remarkable in its composition, not only for its political diversity, but for its inclusion of non-elected citizens.

Its procedure

Public hearings began on November 6, 1990, and were held not only in Montréal and Québec City but in nine smaller centres throughout the province. The Commission had a huge support staff and technical crew to provide live coverage of proceedings. All public hearings were broadcast live, in contrast to the Allaire Committee which held its discussions behind closed doors.

It received in excess of 300 briefs and presentations, and digested hundreds of specialized studies. From the start, the Commission was divided into three groups:

- those supporting outright separation

- those supporting sovereignty association (i.e., political independence for Québec but an economic union with Canada)

- those supporting renewed federalism (i.e., the present system with more autonomy for Québec).

Jacques Parizeau has made it clear that if his party (Parti Québécois) wins the next election, it will declare outright independence. The Liberal Party under Robert Bourassa is torn between federalists and sovereignists, making the Premier's position very tenuous. Bourassa himself (though at time ambiguous) is deemed to be a federalist, as is his senior minister Claude Ryan, who expressed concern about the pro-sovereignty bias on the Commission. By far the majority of presentations favoured some form of sovereignty. After 2½ months of public hearings, the co-chairmen circulated amongst the Commission members a confidential 70-page report reflecting a strong condemnation of the present federal system.

The Prime Minister declined to appear before the Commission to take a stand for the federal government, for which he was criticized by the Opposition in Parliament. Federal Liberal leader Jean Chrétien did make a presentation in which he strongly supported federalism, but he did not receive a very warm reception from Commission members.

The total cost of the Commission was $4.65 million — its relatively low cost being partly explained by the fact that hearings covered only one province and people came to the locations where hearings were held, rather than the Commission doing the travelling.

Its report

In essence, the report (delivered in March 1991) says that Québec will vote on sovereignty by October 1992 unless it receives an acceptable offer for a new constitutional arrangement with Canada. Any such offer would have to be already "binding" on Parliament and the nine provinces. If accepted, the referendum would presumably be unnecessary.

Of the 36 members of the Commission, only four refused to sign the final document, making it virtually unanimous. The earlier Allaire Report also called for a referendum by October 1992, but it seemed to favour further attempts at negotiations. This Commission Report, however, was an ultimatum with a deadline.

There were a number of reactions to the Report. Surveys continued to show strong support by Québecers for some form of sovereignty, yet only half that number were said to be hard-core separatists. It is believed that most Québecers would be satisfied with major changes in the existing federal system. Premier Bourassa made haste to say he regarded the Report as only a guideline. He is a federalist in the sense that he wants to avoid a breakup of the country. By taking that position, he is daring to swim against the tide of separatism, not only within the province but within his own Liberal party. The Parti Québécois was pressing for an immediate referendum in 1991. There is no doubt that the threat of sovereignty gives Bourassa enormous clout in negotiating a political deal with Ottawa.

Ontario Premier Bob Rae and Clyde Wells of Newfoundland reacted by saying that the time-frame was too short, and that Québec has no right to establish deadlines for the rest of Canada.

The Report of this Commission became the official position of the Québec government when it was adopted by the National Assembly. It left the rest of Canada with two options: restructuring the federal system or dismantling the country.

The threat to federalism

The framework of the federal system is described in Chapter 1.

Federalists are those who believe that a strong central government is needed to keep the country together, to cope with its vast geographical area, its small and scattered population, and the economic diversity amongst its various regions.

The opposite view is that the provinces should be given many of the powers currently held by the federal government. The question is how much we can strip the federal government of its powers and still have a country. In other words, we need to define the limits beyond which we cannot go by way of decentralization and still be a viable nation.

The vision in the two Québec reports is of a Canada vastly different from that in place for the past 123 years. If the federal government were to become radically decentralized, it would be unable to take national action in many fields of importance, such as medicare, economic development, native affairs, environment and the arts. We need to determine the essential principles which must be maintained at the federal level in order to ensure equality of national standards in health care and social services, protection of the rights of minorities, preservation of the Canadian Charter of Rights and Freedoms and equalization in regional development. Without these, Canada's distinctiveness as a nation will be seriously impaired.

If Canada were to give Québec most or all of its demands for wider constitutional powers, there could be two results:

• the creation of two Canadas, Québec having vastly more powers than the other nine provinces. This is called asymmetrical federalism (in other words, uneven federalism);

• the other provinces would likely demand similar powers, resulting in massive decentralization.

It must be recognized that any new constitutional structure for Canada must take into account not only the desires of Québec, but also those of natives, northern Canadians, women and minorities. We must aim ultimately, for a Constitution for ALL CANADA, not just for fragmented groups within Canada. This is indeed a complex task, thrust within a narrow (some say, impossible) time frame.

The threat to federalism — as revealed by these Reports — is a reflection of the growing movement in support of sovereignty.

What is meant by Québec sovereignty?

If Québec were to break from Canada, it could take one of three forms:

◆ *Independence* — Québec would become a new and separate nation. This could happen in two ways:

• legally — if Parliament and all provinces agreed, the separation could be in the form of an amendment to the Constitution;

• illegally — in the form of a "unilateral declaration of independence." Such a declaration however carries many risks. For example, when Rhodesia declared independence from Britain in 1965, it was faced with an international trade blockade. When Lithuania declared independence from the Soviet Union in 1990, it resulted in military suppression by Soviet troops. In the U.S.

Civil War (1860-65) the southern states attempted to assert their right to secede; they were prevented by force of arms and the union was preserved. The risk to Québec of a unilateral declaration of independence without approval of the rest of Canada could be the threat of economic reprisals, and possible refusal of recognition by other countries.[8]

◆ *Sovereignty* — This is another phrase often used to denote Québec as an independent autonomous country, having no ties with Canada. It is really no different from independence.

◆ *Sovereignty Association* — Québec would become politically independent but sharing economic ties with Canada, such as the free flow of goods and investment, labour mobility, a common monetary system (currency and banking) a joint postal service.

While it is important to understand these terms because of their frequent current use, it is hoped that it will never become necessary to resort to any of these alternatives. Indeed the thrust of this book is to analyze the issues and search for possible ways of restructuring our country in order to preserve a united Canada. The target date set by the Belanger-Campeau Report — October 1992 — has become the stimulus for accelerated action on constitutional reform.

---

[8]   A unilateral declaration of independence would be illegal under Canadian *domestic* law but Québec might argue that under *international* law it has the right to ''self-determination'' under the United Nations Charter and related Declarations.

INITIAL DELAY

Nothing much happened in the early months following the demise of Meech Lake to allay the nation's anxiety about Canada's constitutional future.

The summer of 1990 was marked by the Oka crisis in Québec when the 77-day standoff by armed Mohawks ended only after Canadian troops were sent to the region at the request of the Québec government. This was done without recall of Parliament, as also was the government's decision to dispatch three battleships to the Persian Gulf in August, and 18 fighter planes in September. These incidents, without parliamentary consultation and coupled with the perceived constitutional crisis, served to further sour the national mood.

The Prime Minister had said, as early as July 27, 1990, that the federal government planned to launch a "major initiative on national unity." Yet no further announcement was forthcoming for several months until the appointment of the Spicer Commission on November 1st, 1990.

CITIZENS' FORUM ON CANADA'S FUTURE
(THE SPICER COMMISSION)

It would have been infinitely better had this Commission been established at least three months earlier, thereby reducing the severe time restraint under which it was obliged to operate. Its creation by the Prime Minister on November 1, 1990 seemed to be timed to distract attention from the Belanger-Campeau Commission which was scheduled to begin hearings in Québec on November 6. Québec quickly denounced the Citizens' Forum and declared it would not participate.

As its name suggests, the general purpose of the Forum was to define the country's future, to identify the values which Canadians share, to provide a vision for change, and to improve the climate for dialogue amongst Canadians. It would ask such basic questions as these:

• what sort of country do Canadians want?

• what kind of country do they think they have?

• what place do they see in it for Québec, for natives, other provinces, bilingualism?

• do Canadians have a common purpose? — if not, there is little point of having a common country.

• do they want their country to continue; if so, in what form?

The Forum was designed to encourage a sense of nationhood through a process of consultation and self-examination. Keith Spicer, its Chairman, would later describe it as a national echo chamber, a prism, to collect and focus Canada's hopes and dreams, a mirror of what is going on in Canadian minds. He saw it as reducing the climate of mistrust among Canadians, encouraging comfortable dialogue amongst people not normally involved in public policy debate. "There is good reason for cynicism," he said, "but better reason for hope." The deadline for its report was July 1, 1991.

There were some who called it a stalling tactic by the federal government; others called it an 8-month wonder with an impossible task; still others said it was an attempt to prepare the country for the expected demands in the Québec Belanger-Campeau Report due in March. Cynics said it was an attempt by the Prime Minister to restore the unity he had helped destroy.

Speaking personally, I fully supported the objectives of the Spicer Commission, and how well in the end it performed its task, and I especially laud the work, vision and optimism which its Chairman displayed in the face of recurring criticism and complaints.

Its structure

The Citizens' Forum consisted of 12 members, five women and seven men, comprising a cross-section of Canadians, including (amongst others) a Newfoundland labour leader, an Indian band manager from northern B.C., a publisher of a French-language magazine in Québec, a Manitoba farmer, a freelance writer, and the head of a provincial Human Rights Commission. Its Chairman, Keith Spicer, was a former newspaper editor, a former Official Languages Commissioner, and for the past year, head of the Canadian Radio, Television and Telecommunications Commission (CRTC).

Its procedure

The procedure for reaching the public took several forms:
- mass meetings with satellite hook-ups connecting several cities, with trained facilitators and moderators provided;
- town-hall meetings across the country;
- small discussion groups in churches, offices, factories, schools, community leagues, institutions, prisons;
- discussion kits mailed out on request containing guidelines, a questionnaire and reporting sheets for groups. Later, 260,000 bilingual kits were mailed out to schools (March 6, 1991) where thousands of students were given a chance to have their voices heard;
- a toll-free telephone hotline with specially trained operators for Canadians to express their complaints and beliefs.

The commissioners held their first organizational meeting in Ottawa on the weekend of November 18, 1990. They came together as strangers to plan the strategy for their monumental task which had to be completed within a very short time-frame (eight months).

Actually, the Commission got off to a very shaky start what with the resignation of two Commissioners within the first few weeks, as well as reported disaffection amongst its administration staff. The Commission was to become a vehicle for the public venting of grievances. Considerable time was obviously needed to clarify its role.

Public meetings

Public meetings began on January 8, 1991 and lasted four months, ending on April 30. At first it was announced that Québec would not be included, but later the Commission decided to hold hearings there even though the Québec government declined to recognize its jurisdiction.

Even before hearings began, Keith Spicer met with nine Western Arctic Eskimos in remote Tuktoyaktuk to symbolize recognition of Canada's first peoples who had crossed the Bering Sea from Asia thousands of years ago.

Equally symbolic was the choice of Saint John, New Brunswick, Canada's oldest incorporated city (1785), as the site of the first official meeting of the Forum. After a public meeting there, the commissioners fanned out through the three Maritime provinces, holding 30 meetings over seven days, listening to what small groups had to say. Newfoundland was dealt with separately at its request. By the end of four months, the Forum had heard the voices of Canadians in every province and territory, expressed in English, French and in aboriginal tongues.

Everywhere the Forum went, there were several recurring themes: complaints about politicians and the rigid political system; doubts about bilingualism; the need for more knowledge before being able to express an opinion. In many places the Forum became a rallying point for gripes and grumbles. Finally, Spicer had to call for solutions rather than a litany of complaints. By early March he was observing that the national consultative process was making people more aware, better informed and more expressive; they were worried about the future and wanted to talk.

The Forum attempted to reach out to the unreachable. It visited a city-centre mission in Vancouver for ex-street people, and later a west-coast prison. It made two trips to Québec — to the small northern community of Chicoutimi on February 7-8; then later all 12 commissioners spent three days in Québec City. On March 20, the Forum issued a preliminary report called "What We Have Heard So Far". It referred to disapproval expressed of government-imposed bilingualism, and of federal funding of multiculturalism; there was support for settlement of native issues and for a relatively strong central government. Mostly, however, people expressed loss of faith in the political system and leadership.

Gatherings were held in the most unlikely places. Spicer himself, dressed in jeans, met with ranchers at a bar in a tiny hamlet in southern Alberta (Manyberries, population 75). Not long after, similarly attired, he met with actors during rehearsals at the Festival Theatre in Stratford, Ontario. With support from the Forum and free airline tickets, the town of Wainwright, Alberta arranged an exchange visit with Marieville, Québec — four residents from each community visiting the other. The last formal meeting of the Forum was with officials and volunteers of international organizations where the focus was on "Canada in the world."

Unfortunately, little interest was shown by francophones in Québec, and native participation was minimal.

Mr. Spicer encouraged other ways of communicating besides verbal. He appealed to poets, artists, orchestras and drama groups to submit items expressing their feeling about the future of Canada. Cartoons, oil paintings, sculptures and poems arrived from across the country in response to the Forum's artistic initiatives. These, together with all records and data collected by the Forum, will eventually be turned over to the Public Archives.

By the time hearings ended, nearly 400,000 Canadians had been heard from, with reports from school groups still to arrive. Sixty-five thousand calls on the telephone hotline, 3,000 letters and briefs, 5,000 individual reports, and some 1,500 more reports from discussion groups were received. When the school reports arrived in mid-May, 300 volunteers were called in to assess them.

As public hearings concluded, Mr. Spicer said he hoped the Forum would wind up as a "modest catalyst for change." It was known to have touched many people deeply. Those who took part were intellectually stimulated and many were emotionally inspired. Most who participated spoke well of the process.

The final report

Released on schedule (June 27), and entitled "Citizens' Forum on Canada's Future," the 168-page report became immediately available in booklet form, with a summary appearing in all daily newspapers, as well as radio and TV releases, a cassette for the blind and a special report for youth.

◆ Part I states that the Forum heard from more than 400,000 Canadians and over 300,000 students — "far more than any other commission of inquiry in the history of our country." All the material was coded under 2,000 key words and studied by professional analysts.

◆ Part II, entitled "What We Heard," lists major issues raised at the hearings. These are examined in detail, accompanied by extracts from citizen comments. The Report contains the following statements:

• The cry heard most often, a cry from the heart, demanded more effective involvement of ordinary Canadians in running the country;

• The Forum acted as a catalyst bringing together, mixing and matching and listening; the process served as a therapeutic exercise in airing grievances;

• (it) was a unique process; it emerged from creative chaos to try to help a country hoping to make sense of itself."

• All through the Report one sees the colourful use of words, the refreshing turn of phrase, and the insightful analysis which are typical of the Keith Spicer style.

◆ Part III, headed "What We Think of What We Heard", states: "We must tell you clearly Canada is in a crisis . . . a crisis of identity, a crisis of understanding and a crisis of leadership" (page 113).

All 12 commissioners signed the report, but two tabled minority reports (pages 141-46): Robert Normand (commissioner from Québec) who criticized the Forum's costs and said it trivialized Québec problems; and Richard Cashin (commissioner from Newfoundland) who said the results were not scientific.

Of major significance is the "Chairman's Foreword" (pages 1-11) written by Keith Spicer himself, essentially a dissenting opinion. He described the Forum as "open-heart surgery on 26 million Canadians." In his view, the Commission Report had not adequately conveyed public displeasure towards the Prime Minister, choosing simply to refer to him as a "lightning rod" for frustrations with politicians in general. Instead, Mr. Spicer stated (page 6), "there is a fury in the land against the Prime Minister," adding that in order to achieve consensus, the Report "understates the displeasure with him." Mr. Spicer says that he himself chose to honour the people of Canada by reflecting accurately what they had said. As Roy MacGregor commented (*Ottawa Citizen*, June 29), "he decided to walk with the people rather than ride with the elite."

These comments are included here simply to show the integrity of the Chairman, who, according to an interview with the *Ottawa Citizen*, underwent tremendous soul-searching before eventually deciding to write this independent opinion.

Quite apart from its dissenting comments, the "Foreword" contains an inspiring message on the spirit of Canada — a literary treasure which is recommended reading for any Canadians who may be doubting their faith in Canada.

References to specific recommendations of the Spicer Commission appear later in this book where relevant.

BEAUDOIN–EDWARDS COMMITTEE ON AMENDING PROCEDURE

This Committee was established on December 17, 1990 by a House of Commons resolution. Its co-chairmen were Senator Gerald Beaudoin (former constitutional law professor at the University of Ottawa), and Jim Edwards (Tory member of Parliament for an Edmonton riding, and a former broadcast executive). It comprised 17 members, consisting of 12 MPs and five Senators. Its mandate was "to consult broadly with Canadians" on the process for amending the Constitution of Canada with particular reference to the role of the Canadian public, as well as possible alternatives to the present procedure. The Committee was required to report by July 1, 1991.

The present amending process, contained in the 1982 Constitution, stipulates that certain types of amendments require the unanimous consent of Parliament and of all provinces, and amendments respecting other subject matters require the approval of only seven provinces having 50 per cent of the population of Canada (explained in detail in Chapter 2 of this book). There is only limited room for bilateral arrangements between the federal government and a province (section 43) since most changes affect other provinces and would require the so-called 7 province/50 per cent approval.

Any changes to the amending process which this Committee might recommend would, under the present Constitution, require the unanimous approval of Parliament and all ten provincial legislatures. Premier Bourassa had already made it clear that Québec would not return to the bargaining table. The anomaly is that the unanimity rule can be changed only by operating within the unanimity rule, that is, all provinces and Parliament agreeing.

The Committee had been furnished by the federal government with a Discussion Paper entitled "Amending the Constitution of Canada." It began its work on February 5, 1991 by listening to the views of 23 political scientists and constitutional experts. It heard from 209 witnesses as well as experts from other countries explaining their amending procedures. It received some 500 written submissions from individuals and organizations. All the hearings were televised, giving Canadians ample opportunity to follow the discussions.

Many of the presentations favoured a national referendum, though opinions differed on the use to be made of the results. There was wide support for a constituent assembly, but little agreement as to its structure. Even while hearings were still in progress, Prime Minister Mulroney expressed disapproval of both these proposals because of Québec's refusal to participate. One would question the propriety of the Prime Minister intervening before the Committee's work was completed. Some people wondered why the government had established the Committee in the first place, while at the same time declaring its position on key issues.

Hearings concluded in early May, and the Committee's 70-page mimeographed report was available by July 1. It is a thorough and readable document. It contains recommendations to enhance public involvement in the process of constitutional change. It adopts an amending formula which would require approval of the Senate and House of Commons, and each of four regions — Ontario; Québec; at least two of the Atlantic provinces; and at least two of the four Western provinces representing at least 50 per cent of the population of that region. The requirement of unanimity would be retained in respect to four subjects only, including the use of the English and French languages, and the offices of the Queen, Governor General and Lieutenant Governors. In essence, this resembles the amending formula in the Victoria Charter in 1971 (subsequently rejected by Québec). In respect to a referendum or constituent assembly, while not endorsing either, it recommended enabling legislation to allow a referendum at the government's discretion, and a Parliamentary Committee on the Constitution — both of which had already been approved by the House of Commons.

It would seem that the government got what it wanted from the Beaudoin–Edwards Committee — policies which it had already endorsed. This does not detract, however, from the diligence and competence with which the Committee pursued its mandate. A more detailed analysis of its recommendations appears where relevant in later chapters of this book.

ADVISORY TEAM OF TOP FEDERAL OFFICIALS

Almost simultaneously with the establishment of the Commissions noted above, the Prime Minister instructed some 40 deputy ministers in the federal civil service, operating in ten teams, to determine what federal powers could be transferred to the provinces and to make recommendations on a redistribution of powers. The Prime Minister indicated that the government would not make public its recommendations.

In addition, an advisory team of top officials in the Prime Minister's Office, including Chief of Staff Norman Spector and Clerk of the Privy Council Paul Tellier, have been working behind the scenes since late 1990 formulating proposals and designing strategies for constitutional reform. As time progressed, it would become more apparent the degree of control these officials would exercise on the direction of constitutional change.

APPOINTMENT OF CONSTITUTIONAL
AFFAIRS MINISTER

When the Prime Minister announced a federal cabinet shuffle on April 21, 1991, he appointed the Right Honourable Joe Clark as Minister of Constitutional Affairs. He was a good choice for the position at a time when the credibility of many politicians had become tainted. He had once been Prime Minister himself (for nine months in 1979), and twice Leader of the Opposition (1976-79 and 1980-83) and during his seven years as Minister of External Affairs (1984-91), he had gained considerable stature. Since the latter portfolio necessitated frequent absences from the country, he was not identified so much with the government's unpopular policies, such as free trade, the GST, Meech Lake, and budget cuts. Also, he was one of the few anglophones in the Cabinet who enjoyed respect in Québec.

Mr. Clark's success in his new portfolio would depend largely on the degree of independence he is allowed in the negotiations he must undertake. In his previous role as Minister of External Affairs, he had a wide latitude to exercise his own judgment and shape government policy without scrutiny from above. In his new role, he must not permit Mr. Mulroney to be seen as masterminding the constitutional agenda. Nor can their old political rivalry be allowed to impede a harmonious working relationship. The Prime Minister wisely used Mr. Clark's greater credibility to achieve a fresh start on the constitution at a time when his own rating in public polls stood at 14 per cent.[9]

Clark began his new job in early May by travelling across the country to visit all the provincial premiers and territorial leaders. He also met with both opposition leaders (Jean Chrétien and Audrey McLaughlin), and though he rejected their suggestions for a national referendum and a constituent assembly, he showed a willingness to listen and to consider. He announced his constitutional plan in the form of a three-way approach:

- to involve as many people as possible in the process;

- to develop a working arrangement with provincially-elected officials;

- to put a political stamp on the work already done by government officials.

Canadians are confident Mr. Clark will bring to his new task a blend of firmness, flexibility and imagination.

---

[9] The Mulroney-Clark career rivalry dates back to 1976 when Joe Clark defeated ten candidates (including Mulroney) for the Tory leaadership. Soon after that, it is well known that Mulroney became the leading architect in a quiet campaign to unseat Clark from the leadership, which ended with Mulroney replacing Clark as Tory leader in 1983. With the Tory general election victory in 1984, Mulroney became Prime Minister and appointed Clark as Minister of External Affairs, resulting in minimal direct contact between them during the following seven years. It is rather ironic that Mulroney might now be looking to Clark to salvage his own political career.

8

PROVINCIAL AND OTHER STUDIES

While federal government committees were at work on the constitution, studies were also being done in other parts of Canada by provincial governments, professional bodies, interest groups and independent organizations, presenting a variety of views on the direction of constitutional change.

PROVINCIAL AND TERRITORIAL GOVERNMENTS

Throughout 1991, most provincial governments set up task forces, study groups or legislative committees to formulate proposals on the constitutional future of Canada. In most instances, the membership on such committees consisted entirely of politicians (Ontario, B.C., Alberta, Manitoba), while others included private citizens as well (New Brunswick, Nova Scotia). Most groups held public hearings and some have tabled interim reports. Newfoundland Premier Clyde Wells expressed some reservations lest these committees have a divisive effect by promoting a narrow provincial viewpoint on constitutional reform rather than a national perspective. Nonetheless a number of creative ideas have emerged, albeit some with a strong provincial orientation. The most recent committee was set up in early July 1991 by the Northwest Territories Legislative Assembly to be composed of six members selected by local leaders to draft constitutional proposals for the Western Arctic.

PRIVATE ORGANIZATIONS

• Canadian Bar Association — set up a Task Force on the Process of Amendment. Each of its five members has been allotted a specific topic of research — its final report is expected before the end of 1991.

• Network on the Constitution — a private group with 15 members, mainly academics and former public servants, based at the University of Ottawa, including such noted personages as Peter Russell, Gordon

Robertson and Michael Bliss. The purpose which they have set for themselves is to analyze the multitude of reports of committees and task forces across the country. They publish a monthly newspaper which is impressive for its objectivity in dealing with controversial issues.

• Business Council on National Issues — sponsored a symposium in Toronto on January 16, 1991, followed by the publication of its two-volume report entitled "Canada's Constitutional Options." This report contained papers prepared by independent scholars, economists, political scientists and lawyers: it is an excellent and comprehensive collection. Additional studies are to follow.

• The Group of 22 — based in Montréal, comprising 22 men and women from many parts of Canada, some in business, some in universities, many having been active in government and politics. Their 28-page report, released in June 1991, entitled "Some Practical Suggestions for Canada" was the result of monthly meetings held between December 1990 and the following May. Though not all its 28 recommendations deserve endorsement, it is an astute and concise analysis, worthy of careful consideration.

• Committee of Native Politicians — This is headed by Liberal Senator Len Marchand (himself a native) to explore the possible creation of aboriginal constituencies for the House of Commons. It does not as yet have any absolute position, and support amongst natives is divided.

• *Maclean's* Forum — Twelve Canadians (six men, six women including one native) representing widely divergent views and without constitutional expertise met from June 7 — 10, 1991, under the auspices of *Maclean's* editorial staff under the leadership of two Harvard University experts on conflict-resolution. Its purpose was to "to pluck the national unity debate from the legislative constitutional pigeonhold where Canada's leaders have kept it." Its report, entitled "To Clarify a Vision," was published in a special edition of *Maclean's* Magazine on July 1, 1991, under the cover story "The People's Verdict."

In summary, all these groups and committees have generated a flurry of imaginative ideas for later consideration.

POLITICAL PARTIES

The various political parties have begun to formulate their constitutional positions, while choosing to remain sufficiently flexible to manoeuvre, depending on the course of constitutional discussions. Briefly, so far as can be ascertained, their positions appear to fall into this pattern:

◆ NDP — at its national convention held in Halifax in June 1991, it supported renewed federalism, an elected Senate, and recognition of Québec's right to decide its own future.

◆ Liberal Party — in its nine-point constitutional reform plan announced April 21, 1991, it favoured a referendum on any new constitutional proposals; it supported a reformed Senate and opposed a constituent assembly because of shortage of time; Québec's position as a distinct society within Canada would be recognized in a preamble to the Constitution, not as an enabling provision.

◆ Reform Party — is opposed to official bilingualism and federal funding for multiculturalism; favours a strong national government with no special status for Québec; supports Senate reform, and the slashing of federal spending on social programs.

◆ Bloc Québécois — supports sovereignty association for Québec and economic ties with the rest of Canada.

We turn now to the federal government's announced plan of action for constitutional reform.

NATIONAL UNITY COMMITTEE

On April 12, 1991, the Prime Minister announced the establishment of a special National Unity Committee, consisting of 18 federal Cabinet ministers selected from the 39-member Cabinet. Its task is to direct and consolidate the federal program for constitutional renewal. Its Chairman is Constitutional Affairs Minister Joe Clark, and the Vice-Chairman is federal Health Minister Benoit Bouchard. It would be working in close conjunction with the team of federal advisors, referred to above.

When Mr. Clark first met with the National Unity Committee on May 4, 1991, he said he was surprised at the amount of work that had already been done. On May 11, the Committee held a six-hour session with the team of federal officials to review the proposals already prepared and which are not scheduled for public release until September. Mr. Clark called it a "substantial document" which the Unity Committee will presumably be reviewing throughout the summer. It is obvious that a draft federal position had already been prepared, though the public had not been informed as to any matters under discussion.

The task of the National Unity Committee is to prepare by September a "Proposal for Constitutional Reform" based on all the available reports. This proposal will be passed on to the Special Joint Parliamentary Committee.

SPECIAL JOINT PARLIAMENTARY COMMITTEE

The announcement of this Committee was made in the Speech from the Throne on May 13, 1991, and its establishment was approved by Parliament on June 21.

The committee consists of 20 Members of Parliament and ten Senators (to be appointed during the summer). In September it will receive from the Unity Cabinet Committee the proposals for constitutional reform. These essentially will have been designed by top federal civil servants and approved by the all-Tory Unity Cabinet Committee. It is expected to contain two parts: one stating government policy and the other outlining options with their implications, for further discussion and debate.

The role of the Parliamentary Committee will be to take the plan across Canada for hearings and consultations, allowing for amendments but aimed at achieving a consensus. By February 1992, the Committee is to prepare a final report entitled "A Plan for a Renewed Canada" which will apparently be Canada's final constitutional proposal.

Under this procedure the final process of debate and decision-making will be entirely under the control of parliamentarians, including unelected Senators, with no membership representation from the general public — on either the National Unity Committee or the Parliamentary Committee. It would have been much more desirable had the federal government chosen to include a few ordinary citizens, as well as specialists in constitutional law, since this is a highly technical subject requiring specialized knowledge beyond what can be assumed in average politicians. By way of a comparison, it is not likely we would allow politicians to decide on medical procedures in brain surgery or organ transplants (for example) without having medical experts on the team; still less should this be allowed in constitutional matters affecting the country's future. In these sensitive times when the public has less confidence in politicians, the Parliamentary Committee could be seen as adhering to the political agenda of its majority. True, the plan is to have the Parliamentary Committee conduct hearings across the country as well as exchange views with its counterparts in the provinces and with provincial legislatures, but the latter groups, like the Parliamentary Committee itself, will be composed almost entirely of politicians.

As far back as May 18, 1991, NDP Leader Audrey McLaughlin expressed concern about the composition of the Parliamentary Committee, urging that the majority of its members should be non-politicians, that in this way it might serve as a kind of miniature constituent assembly for which Canadians had expressed strong support. However, Mr. Clark insisted that politicians must retain sole control over the national unity debate in order "to reassert the role of Parliament in constitutional reform."

Some people will argue that the most important rule of government is that representative democracy must always prevail — that only duly-elected politicians can speak for people in a democratic society. Others would argue that these are not normal times, that Canada is in crisis and that the orthodox principles are no longer adequate to satisfy the expectations of citizens. There is the added point that the present members of Parliament came to power in 1988 before Canada's constitutional crisis reached a crescendo over Meech Lake in 1990. Some people would say that the present government should seek a new electoral mandate before entrusting to politicians the sole decision-making authority relating to the future of Canada.

It is to be noted that one-third of the members of the Belanger-Campeau Commission on Québec's constitutional future were non-politicians.

For some reason, the federal government in the present situation is reluctant to relinquish political control over the process, while presenting a facade of citizen participation. The failure to include non-politicians on the Parliamentary Committee may well prove to be the fatal flaw in an otherwise sensible process. This concern is not alleviated by having advisory panels attached to the Committee, since they would have no vote.

FEDERAL STRATEGY

The process as outlined above would allow some four months of hearings by the Parliamentary Committee, culminating in its final report in February 1992.

Some valid concerns were raised by Liberal Leader Jean Chrétien about the undue prolongation of the process, preferring instead an earlier settlement of the nation's constitutional crisis. While offering his cooperation to the government on constitutional reform, Mr. Chrétien questioned the necessity of a go-slow policy — if for no other reason than that the public is weary of public forums and cross-country commissions. He has suggested instead that the Parliamentary Committee could wind up its work sooner, and a referendum on the final constitutional package be held in early 1992.

If approval of a final proposal is delayed till near the Québec deadline of October 1992, an air of crisis could be fomented so that a federal election in early 1993 would be fought on a single emotional issue (just as was the 1988 election on the single issue of free trade) — all of this to the exclusion of other pressing national concerns deserving the attention of the electorate. If the government were to present to voters a constitutional plan (whatever its terms) and equate its approval with survival of the country, it could elicit enough support on that issue alone to be returned to power. This has raised suspicion in some minds that the agenda for revamping the constitution may be all part of a re-election strategy. This writer would like to think otherwise, but this is a possibility that cannot be overlooked.

SUMMARY

In raising the above concerns — namely, exclusion of citizen membership in the Parliamentary Committee, and a time table having possible political overtones — the purpose is not to discredit the Mulroney government, but to inject an element of public caution as negotiations unfold in the months ahead.

The Mulroney government has been consigned a very difficult task of restructuring Canada's federal system — however much the process may have been mismanaged. Whether any other government or political party could have done better will never be known — for we are a very divided country and becoming ever more difficult to coalesce. Whatever proposals are presented, we must judge them on their merits and not oppose them simply because the government promoting them may be unpopular. To the extent possible, we do need to cooperate with and support those who now have the ominous responsibility of determining the course of our future. As citizens, we must not add to the problem, but at the same time be alert to the subtleties.

We turn now to examine some of the issues which will be requiring decision, and which deserve careful reflection on the part of all Canadians.

10 OUTSTANDING ISSUES

SENATE REFORM

In the current concern for national unity, Senate reform has become central to constitutional restructuring. The pressure for reform comes from the less populous regions of Canada (mainly the Western and Atlantic provinces), and is rooted in feelings of alienation from national decision-making. Reform is seen as necessary to redress the perceived imbalance that exists due to the population domination of central Canada.

There are those who would advocate that the Senate be abolished altogether. According to the Spicer Commission, it should either be abolished or fundamentally reformed, though no preference was expressed. If abolished, the result would be a single House of Parliament with unrestricted legislative powers and no second chamber to review possible hasty or unfair legislation. If we favour abolition, it is not enough to object to the present Senate or how it operates, we must object to the institution itself. On the assumption that most Canadians are interested in a reformed Senate, these comments will explore changes and improvements, rather than Senate abolition.

The focus of reform should address the following questions:

• How should Senators be chosen?

• How should Senate seats be distributed?

• How can the Senate's role be strengthened?

Advocates of the so-called Triple-E Senate would answer these questions with their three-word phrase: elected, equal, effective.

How should Senators be chosen?

The Canadian Parliament consists of the elected House of Commons, which now hasving 295 seats, and the appointed Senate, normally with 104 seats. Both Houses were created by the Constitution Act of 1867. The original purpose of the Senate was to provide a chamber of "sober second thought" and to address regional needs.

All Senators are appointed by the federal government. Many (though not all) are connected with political patronage — a fact that has become the main criticism against the Senate in its present form. As far back as 1874, there was talk of reforming the Senate, followed ever since by continuing demands and proposals for change — a recent example being a Joint Parliamentary Committee in 1984 which recommended Senate elections.

A number of proposals for choosing Senators are currently under discussion. One method is based on the German model of the Bundesrat, under which Senators would be appointed by the provincial *governments* — a method for which Constitutional Affairs Minister Joe Clark has expressed a preference. This would simply mean, however, that political patronage would be shifted from the federal to the provincial level — which would likely be equally unacceptable to most Canadians.

A second method of selection is termed "indirect election" — that is, having Senators chosen by provincial *legislatures* (similar to India and Malaysia). The third method is by direct election as in the United States and Australia. An elected Senate is part of the Triple-E package, and is being promoted as a kind of panacea for Canada's problems.

Several factors deserve consideration in regard to an elected Senate. Because any election (whether municipal, provincial or federal) entails costs beyond an individual's capabilities, candidates in a Senate election would similarly require the backing of a political party. Hence all Senators would arrive with a political label firmly in place, and they would not likely put regional interests ahead of political affiliations on which they depend for re-election. Even now, though Senators are appointed from different regions (wherever the vacancy occurs), when it comes to voting they are influenced more by their political allegiance than by regional loyalties. If the electoral process were to be in effect under a system of Senate elections, the partisan influence would be even more pronounced. It would be naive to assume that having an elected Senate would ensure a greater regional voice.

If Senators are to be elected, several factors must be considered. If they are to hold office for a fixed term and for a longer period than members of the House of Commons (both of which would be improvements), Senate elections could not be held at the same time as general federal elections because of the uncertain timing of those elections. There is also added uncertainty in that a government can be defeated at any time by a non-confidence vote. Canada has had several short-term governments (1957-58; 1962-63; 1979). Though an extra election would add to the cost, it would improve the system, allowing that Senate elections be held at a fixed date every four years. Senators could hold office for, say, eight years, with half being elected each time. Their eligibility for re-election would have to be considered, or alternatively the eight-year term might be considered the maximum.

How should Senate seats be distributed?

The 104 seats in the present Canadian Senate are distributed on a roughly regional basis (24 to each of four regions) in the following manner:

Ontario	24
Québec	24
Maritime provinces	24

(10 each for Nova Scotia and New Brunswick, 4 for P.E.I.)

Western provinces	24

(6 each for B.C., Alberta, Saskatchewan, Manitoba)

Newfoundland	6
Yukon and N.W.T.	1 each

Despite complaints, this distribution does provide a measure of population equality — seven million Western Canadians have 24 seats, as does Ontario with nine million people and Québec with six million. However, this allotment of seats has apparently failed to address regional problems. The task now is to find a method more likely to succeed.

Advocates of the Triple-E Senate propose that each province have the same number of Senators. This would have a number of implications. For example, Prince Edward Island with 1 per cent of the population would have the same number of Senators as Ontario with 34 per cent of the Canadian population. In other words, equality would require Ontario's nine million people with 70 times the population of P.E.I. (120,000) to have the same number of Senators.

It is of interest to note, however, that both the United States and Australia have similar disparities in population, yet both have equal state representation in their Senate.

In 1988, Australia had a 76-seat Upper House, 12 Senators being elected from each of the six states and two from each of the two Territories. The United States elects two Senators from each of the 50 states. In Australia the most populous state (New South Wales) has six million people and the least populous (Tasmania) has only one-half million. A similar disparity exists in the United States between California with over 25 million people and the State of Alaska with one-half million people. The population imbalance in both these countries is comparable with that in Canada.

For this reason, Canada could perhaps follow a similar equality pattern for the provinces and Territories, except for one complicating factor, namely the situation in regard to Québec. Understandably, that province would oppose a reduction from its present 24 Senators, representing 25 per cent of the total Senate to an equality level of only 10 per cent. Somehow, that 25 per cent level has to be preserved in a reformed Senate, in recognition of Québec's distinct language, culture and laws. Hence a possible system of representation for Canada might be along the following lines:

9 provinces, 6 each	54
2 Territories, 2 each	4
Natives	2
Québec (25 per cent of the above total of 60)	15

Total number of Senators   **75**

This would mean that while most provinces had six Senators, Québec would have 15 of the 75. The question is: Would Québec be satisfied? Would the other provinces be agreeable? Critics might say this creates first and second-class provinces. However, there may be no alternative if we are to recognize Québec's unique position. Other proposals can no doubt be devised. This is but one example of an attempt at equality while acknowledging Québec's need for special recognition.

An alternative basis for distribution of Senate seats, and one frequently suggested, would be to replace provincial representation with regional representation. Four senatorial regions would be created (Western, Atlantic, Québec and Ontario), each with an equal number of Senators (say eight each), plus four native representations totalling 100 Senators in all. However, this is not unlike the system currently in effect (described above) which, despite its regional structure, has not overcome the perceived inequities.

The performance of the present Senate

Under the present Constitution, the powers of the Canadian Senate are the same as those of the House of Commons except that the Senate cannot introduce money bills. Unlike the Commons where the political majority frequently cuts off debate by invoking closure, the Senate can deliberate on a bill as long as it wants. In its effort to improve legislation, it need be in no hurry provided it adheres to Senate rules. Indeed, it often conducts nation-wide hearings which may have been denied in the Commons (as with the GST Bill). The only time-restriction for the Canadian Senate is the 180 day limit in relation to constitutional bills.

If the Senate amends a bill which has been passed by the House of Commons, the amended bill is sent back to the Commons, and is again voted upon there. Either the suggested amendments are accepted by the Commons (as happened with the Unemployment Insurance Bill), or rejected (as happened with the GST Bill). But if rejected by the Commons, the bill as finally passed by the Commons must be returned to the Senate for final approval before being presented to the Governor-General for royal assent.

When the Senate revamps these bills, even if the government chooses to reject the suggested amendments, the Senate has performed a worthwhile service. In the end, however, the will of the elected House of Commons prevails, thereby confirming the principle of democracy.

Though the Senate has often been the target for criticism, it has on several occasions reflected public displeasure with bills passed by the House of Commons. In 1988 the Senate refused to approve the Free Trade Agreement unless an election were held (which it was). During 1990, several unpopular measures — the Goods and Services Tax

Act, the "clawback" on seniors' pensions and family allowances, amendments to the Unemployment Insurance Act — were all delayed for upwards of eight months, during which time the Senate was the only political voice symbolizing public discontent. It was only when the Mulroney Government appointed eight additional Senators — under a never-before-used section (26) of the 1867 Constitution — that a Conservative majority forced passage of these bills. Another example of Senate intervention concerned the new Abortion Bill, replacing the one previously struck down by the Supreme Court. The new Bill was submitted to a free vote in the Senate on February 2, 1991 and resulted in a tie vote, which means it was defeated (section 36, Constitution Act 1867). Since neither side in the public debate was satisfied with the Bill, the Senate was fortunately able to prevent its passage.

These examples, though rarely acknowledged, illustrate the influence which the Canadian Senate has had on government policy — instances where it became the only political organ reflecting public discontent with government legislation. In practical terms, it may not accomplish much in preventing legislation, since the Commons can overrule the Senate's rejection, but it has helped to focus public attention on relevant issues.

It is important to understand the working of the present Senate before contemplating its reform.

A reformed Senate

Even if we were to have an elected Senate and equality of representation, these changes would not ensure that a reformed Senate is effective. The word "effective" is the third "E" of the Triple-E Senate, and undoubtedly the most difficult to achieve.

Crucial to the Senate's effectiveness is deciding what purpose it is to serve, what its powers should be and its relationship to the House of Commons. Its approach to legislation should be different from, but complimentary to, that of the Commons.

A Triple-E type of Senate would produce two Houses of Parliament, both elected, and in all probability both subject to party discipline. This could have two results. Firstly, if different political parties dominated the Commons and Senate, each party would be seeking to promote its own political ends, which could result in frequent conflict between the two Houses, and even a stalemate in legislation.

Conversely, if the same political party dominates both Houses, an elected Senate might be nothing more than a rubber stamp for the House of Commons.

Examples of both these extremes were evident in Canada at different times during the 1980s, and would not likely disappear with a Triple-E Senate. The conclusion to be drawn is that if party politics dominate the two elected Houses (which seems likely), the weaknesses in the present system will not end, but may become even more pronounced.[10]

Nevertheless, a reformed Canadian Senate — one which is elected and with equality (not necessarily equal) representation from the provinces — could be effective and at the same time preserve to the House of Commons the ultimate decision when the two chambers cannot agree. A reformed Senate could be entrusted with special and binding powers over matters affecting minorities, such a language and culture; over the development and enforcement of national standards, the implementation of inter-provincial agreements, and the review of appointments to federal agencies (these latter subjects being suggested in the Group 22 Report).

Despite the difficulties, Australia has had what is really a Triple-E type of Senate since 1901. Its experience would indicate that, subject to certain limitations, an equal, elected Senate is compatible with our parliamentary system of government. The question is: Is it effective?

Australia has had to incorporate within its constitution an elaborate procedure for coping with a possible stalemate between the two Houses of Parliament. Under its system, elections are normally held

---

[10] Reference might be made here to Canada's only elected senator. In October 1989, the Alberta government held a provincial election to fill an existing Alberta Senate vacancy, even though there was no provision in the Constitution authorizing such an election. All political parties entered candidates. The voters of Alberta chose Mr. Stan Waters, of the Reform Party. It was not until eight months later that the Prime Minister reluctantly made the appointment. A year later (June 18, 1991), two Conservative MPs (from Regina and Vancouver respectively) raised questions in the House of Commons after Senator Waters disclosed that he devoted only 20 per cent of his activities as Senator and the rest to the Reform Party. It was also alleged that he had one of the poorest attendance records in the Senate. Recent press reports (July 1991) say he is suffering from cancer. This is Canada's only experience with an elected Senator. (Edmonton Journal, Ottawa Bureau, June 19, 1991)

every three years for both the House of Representatives and for half the Senate seats. In the event of a mid-term stalemate, both Houses are dissolved, and an election follows for all seats in both Houses. At one time this resulted in seven elections over a period of 14 years, as well as a constitutional crisis in 1975 when the Senate forced the resignation of the Whitlam government. If after an election the deadlock still persists, a joint session of both Houses is assembled for a free vote. With the House of Representatives far out-numbering the Senate (148 to 76), a solution soon emerges. Since 1949, only rarely has the government of the day had a majority of its party members in the Australian Senate. Also, there have been times when small states in the Senate have managed to block major constitutional amendments favoured by the larger states.

Questions may well be asked if the cumbersome procedure in Australia for breaking a deadlock is worth the price of an equal, elected Senate, or even if its effectiveness has been proven by the Australian experience.

On the issue of Senate reform in Canada, there are those who doubt if the necessary political will exists amongst Canadian politicians to effect radical change. Senate reform has no support in Québec and it will be difficult to achieve a consensus elsewhere. Constitutional Affairs Minister Joe Clark announced on June 18, 1991, that he might set up a "mini constituent assembly" on Senate reform, to act in an advisory capacity to the Parliamentary Committee on the Constitution. It would, however, have no voting power in the main Committee.

Proposals will no doubt be forthcoming from many groups in the months ahead. Whether they be in favour of an elected Senate with equal representation for each province, or an elected Senate with more weight for smaller provinces, or a Senate appointed by provincial governments or by provincial legislatures, or a Senate elected by proportional representation, or even for abolition of the Senate altogether — all these ideas have been aired in the past and are likely to be heard again.

From the various alternatives presented here, no magic formula emerges, simply because there is none. It is important however that Canadians ponder the options, and be prepared to participate in some meaningful way in on-going discussions.

BILINGUALISM

Bilingualism in Canada means the ability to communicate in both English and French. Bilingualism became Canada's official language policy with the passage of the Official Languages Act in 1969 (re-enacted in 1988). It provides for equality of English and French in all "institutions" of the Parliament of Canada and the government of Canada, and the right to receive federal government services in either language.[11]

The Act created the office of Commissioner of Official Languages, and Keith Spicer was the first to hold that position. Dr. Victor Goldbloom is the present incumbent. The Act itself was based on the recommendations of the Royal Commission on Bilingualism and Biculturalism (1963-67), which was the most exhaustive study of English-French relationships ever undertaken in Canada.

The aim of official bilingualism was to blend Canada's two main language groups so as to promote greater harmony, mutual under-standing and respect. Public response to implementation of the policy was favourable and enthusiastic, especially among English-speaking Canadians, who in the years that followed boosted adult enrolment in French-language courses, sent their children to French immersion schools, promoted student exchanges with Québec, and formed study groups on national issues. At the same time, French-language radio and television services were expanded, more federal positions were designated as requiring bilingual qualifications, massive subsidies were forthcoming from the federal Secretary of State for francophone (French-speaking) minority groups in English Canada, and substan-tial transfer payments to provinces willing to increase services in French.

Twenty years ago, bilingualism was the dream of achieving a strong and cohesive Canada. Today, as revealed at the Spicer Com-mission hearings, it is the subject of sharp, and at times bitter debate. What has gone wrong?

Part of the answer lies in the population structure of Canada. In round figures (1986 census) of the 26 million people in Canada,

---

[11] Federal "institutions" are defined as the Senate, the House of Commons, the Library of Parliament, any federal court, any board or commisssion performing a government function, government departments and Crown corporations estab-lished under Parliament.

63 per cent (15 million) are English-speaking (anglophones)

24 per cent (6 million) are French-speaking (francophones)

12 per cent (4 million) are classed as "other", having linguistic roots in neither English or French.

It is obvious from these figures that French-speaking Canadians constitute a minority within the dominant English population of Canada. For that reason it is understandable (indeed commendable) that the thrust of bilingualism has been to elevate the place of French within the Canadian mosaic. This has meant strengthening the French-speaking population in Québec (where they are a majority) and guaranteeing language equality to French-speaking Canadians living outside Québec (where they are a minority). Of the six million French in Canada, five million live in Québec and about one million outside Québec.

There is at the same time within Québec, a minority of English-speaking Canadians. Their number is about the same as that of French-speaking Canadians residing outside Québec (approximately 945,000). Normally we would expect that under bilingualism these two groups (English and French) would be treated the same way where they form a minority.

The 22-year history of official bilingualism in Canada has been a mixture of success and failure. The latest available census figures (1986) show that while French has gained strength in Québec, it has lost ground outside Québec, mainly because of assimilation and intermarriage. Despite efforts to reinforce francophone minorities outside Québec, their numbers have fallen to less than 3 per cent in all provinces, other than Ontario and New Brunswick. While French-language services have been vastly extended throughout Canada, they have not generated the anticipated measure of good will amongst Canadians.

On the positive side, outside Québec there were 184,000 English-speaking children enroled during 1988-89 in French immersion schools (where instruction is mainly in French), which figure represents 5 per cent of the eligible population. In the 1986 census, four million Canadians listed themselves as bilingual.

In the federal civil service, it has been the practice since 1977 to pay an annual bonus of $800 to more than 58,000 federal employees who speak both English and French or who occupy bilingual posts. This bonus applies to one-third of the federal work force, and in 1990 it cost $46 million. There has been an increase in the percentage of positions held by francophones in the federal civil service — now 28.5 per cent which is up from 22 per cent in 1965 — which means that the francophone ratio of jobs is higher than the proportion of their population in Canada.

For bilingualism to succeed, it is crucial that there is a commitment on the parts of both federal and provincial governments to make it work, as well as cooperation amongst governments. This lack of political commitment to language equality is the main cause of the current disillusionment with bilingualism.

At the federal level, Ottawa has not taken the necessary steps (as at July 1991) to implement the new Official Languages Act which was passed by Parliament in September 1988. The new Act is important in that it updates the 1969 Act, makes it conform with the Charter of Rights and extends language services in federal departments. Yet despite the lapse of almost three years, the federal Cabinet has yet to approve of the necessary regulations for its operation.

The former Commissioner of Official Languages, D'Iberville Fortier, in presenting his annual report to Parliament in June 1990, criticized the government for being "slower than slow" in implementing the new Act, adding that the government was doing a "poor job" of establishing official bilingualism. In his final report to Parliament in June 1991 on the expiration of his seven-year term, he expressed further displeasure with the federal government and stated that Canada's linguistic scene had deteriorated.

According to the Spicer Commission, official bilingualism is often seen as unnecessary and irrelevant, wasteful and divisive and should be reduced considerably or eliminated altogether (Report, page 68). However, many participants, while expressing major irritants with the current official languages policy recognized the need for the federal government to provide at least some level of minority languages service (Report, page 70).

Not only has the federal government shown ambivalence towards promotion of official bilingualism, but some of the provincial govern ments have shown even less support for the principle. This has been particularly true of Québec, which, over the past 17 years, has enacted a series of laws that offend the principle of minority language rights — Bill 22 (1974); Bill 101 (1977); Bill 178 (1988). These, in combination, have had the effect of severely restricting access to English-language education in Québec, and have declared French-only as the official language to be used throughout Québec, in courts, in business, the professions and the workplace. Various aspects of Bill 101 have been struck down by the Supreme Court of Canada in decisions handed down in 1979, 1984 and 1988.

The position of the English-speaking minority in Québec has been particularly frustrating. They have been subjected to restrictions in the use of their language in everyday living as well as limitations on access to an English education for their children. In addition they have been caught up in endless court battles in an effort to enforce their rights. While the federal government in 1987 spent $18 million to promote French outside Québec, it spent only $2 million to promote English within Québec, even though the two minorities are about equal in size. English-speaking citizens are grossly under-represented in the Québec branch of the federal civil service which operates in Québec. Also, ·in the Québec provincial civil service, English-speaking Québecers have fewer than 1 per cent of the jobs — 380 out of 60,000 (according to Canadian Press, May 17, 1991) — though the government has recently announced plans to rectify this situation. In June 1991, further language educational restrictions were announced by the Québec Department of Education, whereby all new students must enrol in French classes unless they can produce on the opening day of school, written (not just verbal) confirmation from the government Department as to their entitlement to English schooling (itself an already restricted category).

It is ironical that while Québec is preoccupied with promoting French within its own province (even to denial of the rights of its minorities), it is not noted for supporting French minority rights elsewhere in Canada. This was evident in Alberta when francophones there did not have the backing it expected from Québec during its court case over control of French schools (described below). Some say that Québec does not wish the French language to achieve a significant status in other provinces because Québec would then lose its distinctiveness when compared with the rest of Canada.

It is obvious from these examples that the Québec government does not support official bilingualism, which would require it to guarantee language rights to its English minority. In pursuing its language policy, Québec believes collective rights (assuring French language domination throughout Québec) are more important than the individual language rights (English) which may be violated. Québec's attitude is probably the reason Mr. Mulroney has chosen so far not to implement the new 1988 Act.

Turning now from Québec to other provinces of Canada, where the linguistic minority is French-speaking, and the results of the bilingualism policy are indecisive and inconsistent.

In my own province of Alberta, there are 65,000 francophones, representing 2.4 per cent of the provincial population, making this the third-largest French community in Canada outside of Québec. In Edmonton alone, there are 800 students attending all-French schools, the University of Alberta has a separate French campus, and there is currently a movement for establishment of a French college. Alberta receives about $7 million a year from Ottawa for French-language education, the bulk going to immersion programs.

In March 1990, in a landmark decision of the Supreme Court of Canada (re *Mahé*), francophone parents in Edmonton gained the right to manage and control their own French schools. Even though the Supreme Court directed the Alberta government to enact the necessary provincial legislation, it had not done so 16 months later, and according to the Minister of Education was not likely to do so until 1992 at the earliest. The delay has met with sharp criticism from the *Association canadienne francaise de l' Alberta*, which is now contemplating court action to force government compliance with the Supreme Court ruling (*Edmonton Journal*, June 25, 1991).

Some persons have interpreted this delay as indicating a lack of commitment to bilingualism on the part of the Alberta government. They point as well to Bill 60, Alberta's Languages Act, passed on July 6, 1988, declaring English as Alberta's official language, in order to ensure that Alberta laws will be in English only. This was done as a reaction to a decision of the Supreme Court on an appeal from Saskatchewan in May 1988 (*Queen v. Mecure*), which, (on the basis of section 110 of the Northwest Territories Act) would require all Saskatchewan laws to be translated into French. Since Alberta is governed by the same statute, it sought to avoid this requirement by enacting its own language Act. How ironical that this Act prohibiting the use of French had to be itself printed in both English and French — the only one to be found in the Statutes of Alberta. Saskatchewan did much the same when it legislated that the provincial Cabinet would have the power to decide what laws will be translated, and when. Thus, both these provinces made use of legislation to thwart the language requirement of the Supreme Court — motivated no doubt because of the tremendous costs involved in translations.[12]

The story of bilingualism in Canada would, of course, not be complete unless this analysis were expanded to cover its operation in all provinces and the Territories. However, no study of that magnitude is being attempted here. Suffice to say, however, on the basis of the illustrations above, there appears to be an absence of political will on the part of the federal government and of some provincial governments to promote official bilingualism, especially when it conflicts with other political interests.

If indeed bilingualism has failed, it is largely because governments have not been disposed to make it succeed. There may be another factor as well, besides the political, contributing to its apparent failure, and that is what political scientist Kenneth McRoberts of York University calls sociological forces — seeking to implant a vision of Canada which is at variance with the social reality of the country. This means (one presumes) that we are not psychologically orientated to language duality. Another way of saying it is that language use cannot be legislated; it must be needed.

To the extent that the objective of the Official Languages Act was to strengthen language minorities in Canada, the effort appears to have failed.

And so we end up with a federal government unwilling to promote bilingualism for fear of offending Québec; Québec itself more interested in the collective advancement of French than in the individual protection of its minority; and other provinces (including my own) failing to demonstrate any positive feelings for the advancement of bilingualism.

---

[12] New Brunswick is the only officially-recognized bilingual province in Canada. In 1969, the Legislative Assembly passed its own *Official Languages Act*, which was put in force in 1977. Its provisions were later entrenched in the *Constitution Act 1982* (sections 16-20).

As to whether these political views are shared by the general public, polls show that Canadians continue to support bilingualism and minority rights (Statistics Canada, 1991). However, the May 1991 CBC/Globe poll showed that most Canadians (63 per cent) believe bilingualism has been a failure. This does not mean they are opposed to the concept of official bilingualism, only that the Canadian experiment has failed.

As to the future, every indication points to the federal government, in constitutional discussions now underway, to be planning to turn over to the provinces control over language, while maintaining bilingual services in the federal government and its agencies. This entails risks to minority groups because provinces would no longer be required to offer minority language education or bilingual services unless they choose to do so, and certainly some would not so choose. On the other hand, giving powers to the provinces might ease linguistic tensions. We could still be faced with two language solitudes. This might not be the way we wish to go, but it is probably the direction in which we are heading.

Here again, this writer is not offering any definitive answers, but merely presenting factors to be considered when citizens seek answers for themselves.

MULTICULTURALISM

By culture, we mean all the elements that go into the formation of a nation's spirit — its history; its traditions, beliefs and customs; its literature, art and music; its heroes and heroines; its ideals, feelings and ways of thinking. Canadian culture has been enriched over the past one hundred years by immigrants from countries of Europe, the Middle East, Asia, South America and Africa.

The "melting pot" idea (as practised in the United States), means the creation of a new culture through the assimilation and absorption of all ethnic elements in the population.

Multiculturalism, on the other hand, (as practised in Canada) is a kind of mosaic in which all ethnic groups are combined, but each retains its own distinct character. It is more of an accommodation than an assimilation.

Multiculturalism emerged in Canada during the early 1970s as a reaction to bilingualism which had focused exclusively on English/French relations. It was meant to draw attention to the diversity of other ethnic and cultural groups in Canada. The promotion of multiculturalism has become the official policy of the Canadian government and of several provinces. As part of this policy, funding is provided to numerous ethnic groups to maintain and perpetuate their cultural identity. This can have the effect of impeding the development of a distinctive Canadian culture. It can result in what Prime Minister John Diefenbaker deplored 30 years ago — the creation of hyphenated-Canadians — that is, German-Canadians, Italian-Canadians, Ukrainian-Canadians, Japanese-Canadians, Polish-Canadians, Chinese-Canadians.

Two versions of multiculturalism need to be clarified. The first (which Canadians would certainly support), is that all cultures be allowed to prosper and flourish amongst their followers; that nothing in the law be allowed to impede the personal enjoyment and enrichment to be derived from one's ethnic heritage — subject of course to the requirements of good citizenship. The other version (for which there is growing disenchantment), concerns government funding for ethnic programs which tend to divide rather than unite, resulting in a loss of cohesiveness and eventually a fragmented Canadian culture. University of Lethbridge sociologist Reginald Bibby has coined the phrase "mosaic madness" to describe what is happening.

A section in the Constitution Act 1982 refers to the "preservation and enhancement of the multicultural heritage of Canada" (section 27). Though several views have been advanced as to the purpose of this section, it is generally considered to have an interpretive function. This means that Canada's "multicultural heritage" is a factor to be considered under (for example) the Charter of Rights, especially in interpreting the meaning of "a free and democratic society" (section 1).

It is not surprising that multiculturalism is resisted in Québec as being incompatible with the promotion of its distinct French culture.

The Spicer Commission heard many criticisms of Canada's multicultural policies which "focus on citizens origins, celebrating heritage cultures, rather than embracing a uniquely Canadian national character and celebrating our Canadian heritage" (Report, page 86).

This led the Commission to recommend (page 129) that government funding on multiculturalism be spent instead on integration assistance for newcomers to Canada and on combatting racial prejudice.

In the interests of Canadian unity, this recommendation has merit.[13]

PARLIAMENTARY REFORM

Concerns are being voiced that politicians should be more responsive to the will of the people who elect them; that Members of Parliament when voting should not be bound by the party line; that more free votes should be allowed in Parliament on controversial issues. The effectiveness of individual Members of Parliament is considerably lessened when party discipline is the rule. Writing letters to one's Member (as the public is urged to do), can become a worthless exercise.

In the Speech from the Throne (May 13, 1991), the government appeared prepared to ease, if not abandon, party discipline concerning some subjects in the House of Commons. However, just a few weeks earlier (April 11, 1991), it had put through a measure limiting opposition attacks on government policies and restricting testimony before committees to technical arguments. Yet committee hearings are really the only forum for public input into proposed legislation.

Recommendations from *Maclean's* Forum (described on page 66 above) would dramatically weaken the power of all political parties forcing elected representatives to become more responsive to voters. It would foresee an expanded role for Royal Commissions in policy-making, with results turned into draft legislation and placed before the legislatures for debate.

Another view frequently expressed is that governments should seek a specific mandate before enacting programs which were not part of their election platform. Some people even favour a kind of "recall" procedure allowing voters to petition for the recall of a Member who has ignored the wishes of constituents.

---

[13] The need for this is highlighted in a June 1991 article by John Grimond, foreign editor of the *Economist* of London, the most influential magazine in the English-speaking world. In the article, Grimond stated that Canada spends less on helping immigrants to become Canadians than on subsidizing them to remain semi-Canadians.

The Beaudoin–Edwards Committee recommended a change in parliamentary rules to make mandatory the holding of public hearings on any proposed constitutional amendment, such hearings to be held early enough to allow for changes to a proposal.

Also of public concern is the frequent use of "closure" to end debate in the House of Commons. Though heretofore regarded as an exceptional parliamentary tool, it has been used routinely during the past six years to hasten passage of legislation. The effect is to stifle free debate which is the very essence of parliamentary government.

All of these opinions have been expressed in one form or another in the course of public hearings on the Constitution, especially before the Spicer Commission. Its report speaks of loss of faith expressed in the existing political system (Report, page 96) and the anger directed particularly at federal politicians (Report, page 100), which indicates how intolerant the public have become of abuses within the parliamentary structure.

THE SUPREME COURT OF CANADA

Although the Supreme Court is not included in current constitutional discussions, it was a contentious subject in the Meech Lake Accord. The Accord provided that judges be appointed by the federal government (as now) but from individuals nominated by the provincial governments. The danger in this is that if there were the slightest possibility that such nominees would be identified with the political position of the province which appointed them, their judicial independence would be suspect.

The present procedure for appointment, which is wisely not embodied in the Constitution, allows for consultation with law societies, provincial chief justices and others. Its effectiveness is evidenced in the very high calibre of our present Supreme Court judiciary. Should the subject of appointments ever arise again in constitutional discussions, it would be highly undesirable to have provincial governments the sole nominating body for the appointment of judges, as was attempted in the Meech Lake Accord.

THE MONARCHY

Canada's form of government is a constitutional monarchy, and Queen Elizabeth II is our Head of State. She is represented in Canada by the Governor General who is appointed by her on the advice of the Prime Minister. The current Governor General, The Honourable Ray Hnatyshyn (appointed in January 1990), is Canada's sixth Canadian-born Governor General, previous incumbents having been from Britain. The Queen is represented in the provinces by a Lieutenant Governor.

Contrary to common belief, the patriation of our Constitution in 1982 did not sever all ties with Britain; in fact, the final patriation was enacted in the name of Her Majesty as Queen of Canada.

Erosions in the role of the Monarch have occurred over the years. In 1980, "O Canada" replaced "God Save the Queen" as our national anthem, though the latter is retained as the "royal anthem." Our flag no longer bears the Union Jack. Canada Post has replaced the Royal Mail.

Though the status of the Queen is not an issue in the present constitutional talks, it could arise in future. Arguments in favour of abolition of the monarchy are that it is no longer relevant to Canadians, especially those with roots elsewhere; and that it is a link with our colonial past.

However, the Queen is a unifying symbol; she embodies stability and is the personification of centuries of our inherited history. She has the right to warn, the right to advise and the right to be consulted. In this role, she is untainted by even the slightest suggestion of partisan political loyalties.

Québec is detached from the royal family, and at times even hostile, leading some to suggest that the Monarch's role is divisive.

The question is who would replace her as executive head of government — a President (as in the United States), a Chairman (as formerly in the Soviet Union); would he/she be elected, or appointed and if so, by whom and for how long.

For now at least, Canadians would agree that our present Queen radiates an authoritative grace, which in these contentious times is rare and refreshing.

ABORIGINAL (NATIVE) CONCERNS

Background Facts

The dictionary definition of "aboriginal" is "indigenous; existing in a land at the dawn of history or before the arrival of colonists." In Canada, under the Constitution Act 1982, aboriginals include Indian, Inuit and Métis peoples.

Canada's Indian people number approximately 500,000, representing two per cent of Canada's population. About 62 per cent of these (310,000) live on 2,261 reserves and belong to 593 bands; they speak 53 distinct languages. Half the reserves have less than 1,000 people.

Indians living on the reserves are either registered or entitled to be registered in the "Indian Register" in Ottawa and/or on a band membership list. Their affairs are under the control of the Indian Act which was originally passed in 1876. Title to land on the reserves remains in the Crown, though Indians have a right to exclusive use and possession. Based on treaties with the federal government, many reserve Indians are entitled to a number of rights, such as subsidized housing, free dental service, exemption from income tax, sales tax and property tax, and higher education benefits. Each band has a choice of maintaining traditional government or electing its own Chief and Band Council. The Council can pass by-laws regulating such local matters as health, traffic, alcohol use, sports and recreation. Community band funds are held in trust by the federal Department of Indian and Northern Affairs. However, amendments to the Indian Act are now under consideration allowing the bands more control over these revenues. The annual budget for the Department is around $4 billion, yet many reserves have serious economic and social problems: high unemployment, alcoholism, poor health, juvenile delinquency, school dropouts, suicides, family violence, and child neglect.[14]

About 200,000 Indians live off reserves in various communities and urban centres. They are not entitled to the same benefits, other than subsidized higher education, and they do pay taxes.

---

[14] The writer gained first-hand knowledge of these problems, having conducted a monthly circuit court for over ten years near an Indian reserve (reputedly the wealthiest in Canada) while serving as Judge of the Juvenile and Family Courts of Alberta (1966-1983).

The Inuit (called Eskimos until 1939) inhabit the northern regions of Canada, living in small scattered communities. Their total population is approximately 27,000. They speak a common language with a half dozen dialects, and have achieved recognition through their distinctive Inuit art.

Métis are a mixed-race people (part Indian ancestry), some residing in Métis settlements, but most living within the general population. They number about 60,000.

Thus, Canada's aboriginal people are not a homogeneous group of people, but a diverse and scattered population. Many belong to national organizations such as the Assembly of First Nations, the Native Council of Canada, the Métis National Council, and the Inuit Committee on National Issues.

From a worldwide perspective, there are more than 250 million indigenous people, representing four per cent of the global population, living in 70 countries, mostly as minority groups. Their ancestors were the sole original inhabitants of lands which were later colonized by foreigners. Such colonialism began about 1500 AD.[15]

A new international movement is promoting recognition of aboriginal rights. The aspirations of Canadian natives are not unlike those in other parts of the world. Their first claim is to ownership of ancestral lands which they and their ancestors have occupied since antiquity, the rights to which they claim have never been extinguished. Their second, and more recent, claim is for native self-government.

Both issues have become part of Canada's current constitutional talks.

Settlement of Land Claims

To understand the importance of this issue, one needs to understand the significance of land in native culture. Land is not simply a piece of property to be used or exchanged. Native people have a profound relationship with the land; it is central to their identity as a people. They view their land as a source of life, their link with the past, the core of their culture. Aboriginal title, they claim, is inalienable.

Natives in Canada argue that their aboriginal rights were not extinguished because their ancestors were never conquered or defeated in a war; their lands were simply colonized by European

---

[15] "The GAIA Atlas of First People" by Julian Burger, Anchor Books, Doubleday, 1990.

settlers. At one time, not too long ago, natives claimed half the land mass of present-day Canada, including two-thirds of British Columbia and even parts of downtown Montréal and Capitol Hill in Ottawa. Until the early 1970s, the Government of Canada paid little attention to these arguments, assuming on the basis of a Privy Council decision in 1889 that aboriginal title did not exist.[16]

A federal White Paper on Indian Policy in 1969 had advocated an end to any special status for Indians. However, in 1973, the Supreme Court of Canada, in a split decision in the famous Calder case, declared that the Nishga Indians in British Columbia had acquired aboriginal title to lands which had been continuously occupied by them and their forebears from time immemorial.

Following that decision, the federal government set up an "Office of Native Claims" to handle the growing demand for land claim settlements. The process however moved at a glacial pace over the next 15 years, with the Claims Office agreeing to consider only three claims at a time, and requiring that any settlement include an "extinguishment clause" putting an end to aboriginal rights — a condition which many natives refused to accept. The result is that as of 1991, very few "comprehensive land claims" (those involving treaties) have been settled; and many "specific claims" (those based on treaties) remain unresolved.

In the years following the *Calder* case, the Supreme Court of Canada continued the trend it had begun by further defining and reinforcing aboriginal rights, culminating in 1990 with its decision in the *Sparrow* case. That case, involving native fishing rights, held that "only clear and plain language" in treaties and legislation can extinguish native rights; that natives are entitled to a "high standard of honourable dealing;" and that the government is in a fiduciary [acting as a trustee] position in relation to aboriginals. This decision represented a great triumph in judicial recognition of native rights.

Natives however suffered a set-back in 1991 in the *Gitskan* case, involving a claim by two native tribes to title and ownership of a vast area in northern British Columbia. The trial lasted for three years, at the conclusion of which Chief Justice McEachern of the Supreme Court of British Columbia (in a 350-page judgment), held that aboriginal rights do not include ownership of land and jurisdiction

---

[16] *St Catherine Milling v. The Queen* (1899), 14 A.C. 46.

over the territory. Natives complained bitterly that this decision did not comply with the Sparrow case. However, there was this significant difference: while Sparrow dealt with native fishing rights, Gitskan dealt with title to land. Since appeals could take years before a final decision, it may mean that natives, instead of seeking legal remedies through the courts, may feel obliged now to resort to political solutions through negotiations with the government — a process which native people have not found entirely satisfactory in the past.

Perhaps in response to this situation, the federal government, in the Speech from the Throne in May 1991, announced the establishment of an Advisory Board on Land Claims to streamline the process for settlement of "specific" land claims, and set a target date of the year 2000 for settlement of all claims. The Chairman of this Board is Harry LaForme, an Ojibwa from Brantford, Ontario. He is a lawyer who has been Indian Commissioner for Ontario since 1989.

As to the views of the public on this issue, citizens told the Spicer Commission that they regarded settlement of land claims as a top priority; that "these outstanding claims are a national and international embarrassment and must be resolved quickly and fairly" (Report, page 80). The Commission was told repeatedly by groups and individuals in all parts of the country that "people feel very uninformed about aboriginal issues in general, and these issues in particular, and are consequently very reluctant to make specific recommendations" (Report, page 74). "We want more discussion and education," pleaded one group from Nova Scotia.

Little wonder, with a subject as complicated as this and with no consensus as to an appropriate solution. The enigma becomes even more formidable when dealing with the subject of native self-government.

Native Self-Government (Sovereignty)

Native Indian people were not given the vote in federal elections until 1960. The first native elected to the House of Commons was Len Marchand in 1968. He has since been made a Senator. A total of 12 natives have sat in the House since Confederation.

No one really knows what native self-government would mean within the context of the Canadian federation. The dictionary definition of self-government is "administration by a people or state of its own affairs without external direction or interference." This is a degree of independence which is not even accorded to the provinces of Canada.

The Constitution Act 1982 specifically "recognizes and affirms" what is described as "existing aboriginal and treaty rights" (section 35), leaving First Ministers to decide what is embodied in "aboriginal rights," and whether the term includes the right to self-government. Three conferences were held (1983, 1985 and 1987), in an attempt to clarify the issue. All ended in failure.

The argument which native people use in advancing their claim to sovereignty is that before the white man came, Indians exercised control over their lands and people, through a simple form of government based on tradition and customary law. The fact that the Canadian government entered into treaties with the Indians indicates that they were recognized as a political group, as a sovereign people, and negotiations proceeded as if on a nation-to-nation basis. What native groups now want is to have the right to native sovereignty entrenched in the constitution — just as section 35 has entrenched aboriginal and treaty rights. Opponents say sovereignty cannot be entrenched until it is defined; the native position is to entrench it first, and define it later. Herein lies a basic dilemma.

The present 2,200 reserves are small, scattered and geographically separated. If they became independent, Canada would be fragmented into a patchwork of holes resembling a gigantic piece of Swiss cheese. Many questions would arise: Would these new nations be allowed to use Canada's infrastructure (roads, railways, power, electricity), its banking system, currency, postal service, police, courts? Could they levy taxes? Would their citizens be exempt from Canada's criminal law? Would they continue to receive federal funding, on which they are currently very dependent? Since a land base is essential to the formation of any government, settlement of land claims would be a necessary prerequisite to sovereignty.

There is no single model of self-government that could apply to all native people. Since band councils or traditional governments are the only recognized native political units, it would be logical to begin the process towards self-government at those levels. This was the view put forward in 1983 in an excellent report of a Parliamentary Task Force entitled "Indian Self-Government" (the Penner Report). The legislative powers of bands could be gradually expanded to include such areas as economic development, environment, resources, education, training, health and social services, and taxation. Several bands have already acquired some of these powers through arrangements with their respective provincial governments.

Such a system would help natives make the transition from government control under the Indian Act to self-government, allowing each group to plan the system most suited to its historical and traditional values. Band governments might even expand to a regional level where several would be combined, even though geographically separated. A simpler and more realistic approach would be to allow individual bands to apply for self-government through the Department of Indian Affairs which would work out individual systems appropriate to each group.

It must be remembered that not all native groups are interested in self-government or feel themselves capable of administering their affairs if granted the right. Much of the agitation for sovereignty comes from strong native leaders or from reserves with a sound economic base and proven leadership. The fact that natives cannot even agree amongst themselves as to the future of the Indian Act (whether it be repealed, amended or left as it is), indicates the lack of any uniform native policy.

A reasonable view would be that only after an overall plan is established should consideration be given to entrenchment in the constitution of a native right to self-government.

Native Constitutional Demands

Quite apart from native self-government, native groups have made other constitutional demands, including the following:

- the right to be considered one of Canada's founding nations;
- representation in provincial and territorial legislatures;
- a veto power over legislative changes affecting native interests;
- representation on a full and equal basis at conferences of First Ministers;

---

[17] There is currently a Committee of Native Politicians under Liberal Senator Len Marchand, studying proposals for aboriginal representation in the House of Commons. One suggestion is to create nine constituencies across Canada to represent the scattered reserves and urban native populations, giving natives the choice of voting in an aboriginal riding or in the riding where they reside.

• a guaranteed number of seats in the House of Commons.[17]

Not all native groups support all of the constitutional demands listed above.

The Beaudoin–Edwards Committee on Amending the Constitution recommended that any constitutional amendment affecting aboriginal peoples should have the consent of the aboriginal people of Canada. The Committee endorsed aboriginal representation at constitutional conferences, and the holding of biennial conferences to address the rights of aboriginal people.

Ovide Mercredi, Grand Chief of the Assembly of First Nations, speaking to chiefs in the Atlantic region on July 9, 1991, referred to a two-year program for native reform. It would include native self-government, native institutions of government, protection of land, language and resources, which could be achieved (he said) only through a new Constitution. At the same time, other chiefs continue to work with the federal government for changes to the Indian Act, which is a less radical approach with greater possibility of acceptance. Prime Minister Mulroney has stated categorically that the Canadian government will never accede to demands for political sovereignty — "native self government does not now and cannot ever mean sovereign independence."

Recent Favourable Developments Affecting Natives

• Royal Commission on Native Issues — This was first announced by the Prime Minister in Victoria on April 24, 1991, and confirmed in the Speech from the Throne on May 13. Its purpose is to deal with economic, social and cultural matters affecting aboriginal people. It will not deal with political issues, such as self-government, land claims or the Constitution. Former Chief Justice Brian Dickson was assigned to recommend the mandate for the Commission and its membership. Accordingly, Co-Chairmen have been appointed, namely George Erasmus, former Grand Chief of the Assembly of First Nations, and Bertha Wilson, retired justice of the Supreme Court of Canada — along with five commissioners.

• Advisory Board on Land Claims — As described on page 94 above, this is designed to accelerate settlement of native land claims.

• Review of the Justice System as it relates to aboriginals — In June 1991, the federal government promised to begin discussions with the provinces and native leaders concerning alleged injustices towards aboriginals within the justice system. Talks have also begun in several provinces which would give natives a larger role in law enforcement, the court system and administration of justice. In particular, the Ontario government entered into an agreement with its 170,000 native people in August 1991, acknowledging their right to be self-governing. This would, in effect, make native government superior to that of municipalities. In a sense, the Agreement is mainly symbolic, since the federal government retains constitutional responsibility for native peoples.

• Native Participation in Constitutional Talks — An agreement was reached on July 5, 1991 between the Assembly of First Nations and Constitutional Affairs Minister Joe Clark allowing a parallel native process working in tandem with the Parliamentary Committee on Constitutional Reform. Natives will be conducting miniature "constituent assemblies" for their various groups (elders, women, youth and urban natives) with a view to presenting to the Parliamentary Committee a unified set of proposals on native issues. Natives had objected to the earlier plan in which they simply would be included on advisory committees. Even under the new plan, any report from this group would have no official constitutional status but would be in the nature of recommendations only. Nevertheless, this concession does give recognition to a special native role in constitutional reform.

Summary of Aboriginal Issues

Native demands for constitutional reform are not likely to go away: aboriginal peoples in other countries are making similar demands. For Canada, settlement of all issues will be a lengthy evolutionary process. Native people provide the roots to our ancient past; they are worthy of understanding and encouragement as they find their way to a better social, economic and political future.

11 PUBLIC PARTICIPATION:
CONSTITUENT ASSEMBLY AND NATIONAL REFERENDUM

Canadians are demanding a greater role in the process of constitutional change. This is a reflection of the national mood that decision-making on Canada's future must no longer remain exclusively with politicians. Several alternatives have captured the spotlight during public hearings — the most popular being demands for a constituent assembly and a national referendum.

CONSTITUENT ASSEMBLY

The idea of a constituent assembly has a high democratic appeal, but it presents serious practical problems. Who should attend — politicians or lay people or both? How should they be selected — appointed or elected, and if so by whom? What should its role be — to draft a constitution, amend one already made, or to act in an advisory capacity? How would it reach its decisions — by consensus, majority vote or unanimity? What use would be made of its conclusions — submitted to legislatures, endorsed by referendum, or both?

A variety of suggestions have been forthcoming, mainly in presentations to the Beaudoin Edwards Committee. They range from having all delegates selected from provincial legislatures or Parliament (Peter Russell); to having both politicians and lay people selected by provincial legislatures (Bob Rae, Clyde Wells); to having every legislature nominate persons (possibly 3,600 in all) from which a random selection would be made (Estey/Nicholson). The total number of delegates to such an assembly might be as few as 80 (Rae), to as many as 300 (Estey). The challenge would be to create a body small enough to get something done, yet large enough to be truly representative of the people of Canada.

Unless delegates came equipped with some grasp of constitutional law, their role would be difficult indeed. Because they would gather as strangers, time would be required for the assembly to coalesce as a working group. This is something which even the Spicer Commission, with only 12 members, found difficult to attain and may never have fully achieved.

A larger constituent assembly, with its diversified membership undertaking the revision of a complicated Constitution within the rigid time restrictions prescribed by Québec, would find this much more difficult.

A comparison is frequently made to the Constituent Assembly which drafted the U.S. Constitution in Philadelphia in 1787, following the American War of Independence. But that was a first constitution for a new country, not for a country like Canada with over a century of statutes already in place. Those were simpler times in a much simpler society without pressures from competing groups such as we have today. Nor was the Philadelphia assembly a truly representative body: delegates were all white, all male, all Protestant and virtually all lawyers. Meetings were held in secret. The completed constitution was presented to the 13 new states to be accepted or rejected in its entirety (much like the Meech Lake Accord). The assembly was neither representative of the population, nor was its procedure democratic.

Other countries have used a constituent assembly in preparing a first constitution — for example, France in 1791, Australia in 1899, India-Pakistan after World War II, and most recently Namibia and Nicaragua. It is doubtful if it would be workable at this stage in Canada's constitutional evolution.

The federal government made it clear from the beginning that it does not favour a constituent assembly. The reason given is that Québec would not participate, it may also denote a desire on the part of the federal government to retain political control. In his Report, Keith Spicer urged the government to reconsider its rejection of a constituent assembly. The Beaudoin Edwards Committee dismissed the concept, favouring instead a Parliamentary Committee of politicians to review the government's constitutional proposals. This is precisely what the government has done.

Certainly no one would disagree with the concept of a constituent assembly, however great the practical problems. It is unfortunate that we do not have three or four years to adequately test its application to Canada's present constitutional structure. Whatever its deficiencies, the public demand for a constituent assembly will continue to be heard, simply because, for many people, it is their only way of expressing dissatisfaction with the present process. In the words of Angus Reid: "People are grabbing at the idea of a constituent assembly as a kind of life raft."

NATIONAL REFERENDUM

Referendums have been rarely used at the national level in Canada, and never in regard to constitutional issues. Since 1867 there have been only two national referendums — one in 1898 on prohibition, the other in 1942 on military conscription. Both had a polarizing effect on the country, with the majority of Canadians outside Québec voting YES and the majority of Québecers voting NO. Provincially, referendums have been used in a variety of non-constitutional issues — from implementing daylight-savings time to approval of a fixed link to Prince Edward Island. Several countries, including Sweden, Switzerland and Australia, have used referendums to ratify constitutional changes. A number of such proposals have been rejected by voters, particularly in Australia.

Referendums present several challenges, the most difficult being the precise wording of the referendum question: it should never be designed to achieve a particular result. The timing of the vote must avoid periods when feelings are inflamed. The public must be furnished with unbiased information concerning the issues. The media must be objective in its coverage of the referendum debate. Business interests must not be allowed to manipulate public opinion by using costly advertising to promote a particular viewpoint. Minority interests need to be protected to avoid what Peter Russell calls "the tyranny of the majority." A referendum has the effect of freezing public opinion as at the date of the vote, allowing for little flexibility should conditions change. Even more difficult is the interpretation to be given to the results. Would an overall majority be sufficient for approval, or should the voting be weighed according to regions?

Whatever the results, a referendum alone could not amend the Constitution. Under present law, amendments require ratification by Parliament and a given number of provinces, depending on the subject matter. The Trudeau government in 1978 introduced a bill to allow referendums in constitutional matters, but the bill was never passed. The Beaudoin Edwards Committee on Amending Procedure did not recommend entrenchment in the Constitution of a ratification referendum. It did however recommend enabling legislation to allow the government, at its discretion, to hold a referendum. But the results were to have no legal weight and would not be binding on the two levels of government. In other words, it would be an advisory mechanism only. This is, in fact, what the government had already done.

The Spicer Commission preferred to leave the matter to experts for further study. However, the Southam Unity Survey of June 1, 1991 showed that 73 per cent of Canadians outside Québec favoured a national referendum.

Conservative M.P. Patrick Boyer, in his book "Lawmaking by the People," believes that a referendum is a critical element in reforming the country. He has made this comment:

"We Canadians have not been participants in our political system so much as spectators to it. Canada has been a very timid democracy, with a political establishment that refuses to trust the people to make major decisions, even though it is the people who have to live with the consequences of those decisions."

Judging from the mood of the country in mid-1991, Canadians are not likely to be satisfied with anything less than a national referendum on any final constitutional package.

THE POPULIST MOVEMENT

Populism is a new development in Canada. Though it has no structure or organization, it is the doctrine of citizen empowerment, the belief that individuals can make a difference. Simply stated, it means people having a say in what happens to the country. As British Columbia political scientist Alan Cairns has said, "Governments are no longer the sole inhabitants of the constitutional playing field."

At the Forum conducted by Maclean's Magazine in June 1991, one of the leaders, Harvard Law Professor Roger Fisher, made this comment:

"Citizens need not wait for their leaders. Individual citizens of Canada, individually as well as collectively, can probably make a far greater difference than they assume ... Be creative. Work with others, using your collective talents, experience and points of view."

Though the populist movement may have no clear focus as yet, the voices of individuals are likely to be heard more frequently — alone or in unison with others — confident, assured and decisive. It is something in which any Canadian with positive and constructive views can participate.

12

RESTRUCTURING OF CANADA: THE OPTIONS

The constitutional structure of Canada has been federalism through-out the 124-year history of the country. This means there are two levels of government — federal and provincial — each having specific legislative powers allotted under the Constitution. With our present system now under review, we need to examine other options and possible alternatives.

ASYMMETRICAL FEDERALISM

This is a term meaning not the same, not equal. Some see it as a fancy expression meaning special status for Québec. Under this system, Québec would be given greater powers than the other provinces. The result would be inequality.

The question is: Would the other provinces agree? Or would they demand the same powers for themselves? If so, Canada might end up as ten autonomous fiefdoms. During Meech Lake discussions, most of the nine provinces demanded equivalent powers to those being sought by Québec. This is akin to the principle of "juridical equality."

Under a system of asymmetrical federalism, Québec would retain seats in the Canadian Parliament and be able to influence decisions affecting the rest of Canada. However, Canadians outside Québec would have little say in the affairs of that province.

Most Canadians would not object to Québec having legislative control over matters related to its language, culture, and laws, as well as administrative control over other areas of federal jurisdiction. However, sufficient powers must remain with the central government if Canada is to be preserved as a unified nation.

In a sense, asymmetry has always been part of Canada's relation-ship with Québec. At the time of Confederation, Québec was granted special language protection. To this day, Québec retains its own Civil

Code which differs from the English common law. In addition, special agreements in recent years have given added powers to Québec in such fields as pensions, immigration, tax abatement, health services, and shared-cost programs.

It could be that a system of asymmetrical federalism, wherein Québec had greater powers than other provinces, would be an inducement for Québec to remain as part of Canada. However, nations founded on the principle of inequality are known to be inherently unstable. While Canadians would be willing to make concessions to Québec in recognition of its unique character, a limit must be placed on the extent to which the equality principle can be compromised.

The concern would be that while asymmetrical federalism might reconcile Québec, it could undermine the essence of Canadian federalism.

REGIONALISM

This is the plan promoted by Professor Thomas Courchene, Director of the School of Policy Studies at Queens University, in his presentation to the Belanger-Campeau Commission. Under this plan, Canada would be divided into five regions: Québec, Ontario, Canada West, Canada East, and a combined Territories and First Nations region.

Each of the five regions would be represented equally in a revamped Senate, to be called the Federal Council. Each region would decide on how to select its members — by election, appointment or a combination of both. The plan is meant to give greater regional autonomy through a modified Upper House.

In the legislative field, certain powers would be assigned to the federal and provincial governments, with the remaining powers being concurrent — each province would choose which powers it wished to exercise and which powers it wished to leave to the federal government. In this way, Québec could have access to all powers immediately and the other provinces could choose to proceed more slowly into the concurrent area, or perhaps not at all. This would ensure a more flexible division of powers.

This proposal, while complicated, appeals to many Canadians.

The underlying assumption in regional representation is that regions are a homogeneous bloc within themselves. This is not necessarily true amongst the provinces of Atlantic Canada or of Western Canada. At the Western Canada Premiers' Conference, held in Nipawin, Saskatchewan on May 12-13, 1991, the premiers managed to achieve only an occasional joint position, since most were concerned more about their own province than about the region. One reporter in attendance, Mark Lisac of the *Edmonton Journal*, said: "The illusion that the West would speak with a powerful united voice was shattered."

Regional federalism, to succeed, would require a fairly high level of unity within the regions themselves. This is by no means assured.

DECENTRALIZATION

Decentralization means taking away certain powers from the federal Parliament and giving these powers to the provinces. The provinces could make certain laws and administer certain programs which until now have been under federal control. As a result, the provinces would have enhanced powers at the expense of the federal government, which would be less able to take responsibility in matters of national importance.

The movement to decentralization has always been strongest in Québec, though at times in the past, pressure has come from certain other provinces (particularly in the West) for greater provincial autonomy. However, from a recent listing showing provincial constitutional priorities (published on July 23, 1991) Alberta is the only province, apart from Québec, listed as strongly favouring decentralization. Most of the other provinces (including Manitoba, Ontario, New Brunswick and Newfoundland) favour a strong central government — modified, though not weakened. The official position of the Alberta government has favoured greater powers to the provinces. However, when public hearings were held throughout that province in May 1991 before the Legislature Committee on Constitutional Reform, by far the greatest number of written and oral submissions supported a strong central government.

Other provinces, particularly in Atlantic Canada, fear that decentralization will force them to assume responsibilities beyond their financial means, leading to forced curtailment in the level of social and economic programs which they can offer their residents. This could lead to a fragmentation of Canada into have- and have-not provinces and an end to national standards which have been a strong unifying force throughout the country. There is a certain contradiction between talk of a united Canada and support for decentralization.

Despite these factors, indications are that the federal government is moving in the direction of a vastly decentralized federal structure. The Advisory Team of senior federal officials has been engaged for months in identifying legislative powers that can be transferred to the provinces. Decentralization will undoubtedly be a major part of the federal constitutional package to be released in September 1991.

As an indication of the trend in federal thinking, a request recently came from Communications Minister Perrin Beatty to a coalition of Arts groups, asking their advice as to national cultural programs which could be handed over to the provinces in a new constitutional deal. The Canadian Alliance for the Arts stated as follows in its reply to the Minister:

"We cannot have national unity without national culture. What is required is a strengthening, not weakening, of national policies in all areas of culture and the arts."

Québec has demanded complete control over cultural matters. The Arpin Committee Report to Québec's Minister of Culture, delivered in June 1991, proposed that all responsibility for culture in Québec should lie with the Québec government. However, several other provinces, including Ontario, Nova Scotia and Prince Edward Island, have stated they do not want more control over culture.

An inconsistency is apparent in the federal government's position on decentralization. After speaking for months in support of such a policy, the Prime Minister announced, in the Speech from the Throne in May 1991, that federal initiatives would be taken in the fields of education and domestic trade — both being matters within provincial jurisdiction. On May 29, 1991, the creation was announced in the House of Commons of a federal Ministry of Regional Development for Québec, to which objections were also raised, alleging intrusion in a field of primary provincial jurisdiction. All of these announcements seemed ill-timed, when the division of powers is on the constitutional agenda.

If there is to be a transfer of powers, it should be a two-way process — not only more powers to the provinces, but a transfer as well from the provinces to the federal government. There is a compelling argument that responsibility for such fields as health care, higher education, social welfare and the environment should rightly be vested in the federal government as a sure way of maintaining equality of standards and uniform accessibility to benefits. These and like powers could be placed under federal legislative jurisdiction, and administered by the provinces. However, in all likelihood, the trend in federal planning is in the opposite direction.

Other more subtle forces are at work in bringing about decentralization. Over the past year, the federal government has been cutting back on the transfer payments it makes to the provinces. These are shared costs for health care, higher education, social welfare and unemployment insurance. Shifting responsibility and control to the provinces over such programs is in effect drifting towards decentralization. It is being achieved through the fiscal system without resort to constitutional amendment.

Lastly, in the field of international affairs, excessive decentralization would detract from the image of national solidarity that Canada must present to the world. This is particularly important in the current trilateral talks with Mexico and the United States over free trade. During the course of these negotiations, the United States has threatened to re-open the Canada-U.S. Free Trade Agreement to challenge Canadian autonomy over such matters as culture. The Canadian government must not be perceived as a weakened federation, lest there be further incursions of this nature on Canadian sovereignty.

It is essential that adequate powers remain at the federal level if we are to survive as a nation. This is why decentralization represents such a threat. Though some decentralization is inevitable, the crucial factor is the degree of decentralization which should be permitted. We must determine the maximum transfer of powers to be allowed — and nothing more.

RENEWED FEDERALISM

Federalism is the system under which Canada has functioned since 1867. Renewed federalism refers to changes and adjustments which are perceived as necessary to Canada's federal system in order to adapt it to changing conditions and circumstances.

The essential feature of federalism is the division of powers between the levels or orders of government.

In the course of Canada's century-long evolution, the ideal of equality amongst all the provinces gradually became eroded due to differences in the economies of various regions. To offset these disparities, and to provide a measure of equalization, federally-sponsored programs were instituted to assure to the weaker provinces the same benefits as the stronger ones. Out of this policy came such programs as regional development, equalization payments and a national network of social security — all based on the relative needs of different areas and their resources. This is a product of federalism, and it has enhanced the bonds of nationhood.

What is being questioned today is the constitutional structure of Canadian federalism, and our strategy of equalization. In seeking answers, our aim must be to change the nature of federalism, but not to destroy its essence. The renewed structure will contain elements of both asymmetry and decentralization — the challenge will be to assimilate all components into a new constitutional framework acceptable to the scattered regions of Canada and protective of minorities. To achieve this objective, we must resolve conflicting pressures from interest groups, and reconcile provincial demands. This will call for the utmost goodwill amongst competing interests, and an unselfish commitment to the preservation of Canada.

The Report of the Spicer Commission sets out in these colourful words, the challenge of renewed federalism:

"The crafters of a new federation, like the original Fathers of Confederation, will be called on to be bold, imaginative, and determined to let nothing stand in the way of a responsible, honourable compromise acceptable to all the federation's members." (Report, page 119)

Public opinion polls, both within and outside Québec, confirm that of all the constitutional options, renewed federalism is the preferred choice of Canadians.

JOINING THE U.S.A.

The comment is often heard that parts or all of Canada should join the United States — now or in the event that Canada breaks up. The idea is really quite laughable, for the simple reason that the United States would not have us. Already the United States has control of our resources, and to a large extent, our economy — as a result of the Canada-U.S. Free Trade Agreement. Why, we might ask, would they choose to take on our political problems? Would they wish, for example, to have Canadians sit in the U.S. Congress? In truth, the United States has obtained all it needs or desires from Canada, thanks to the Free Trade Agreement.

Suppose, however, that some portion of Canada decided it wished to become part of the United States. The procedure that it would follow is interesting. The break-away region would have to start out under the U.S. flag as a territory or commonwealth, without any guarantee of it becoming a state in the near future or even at all. This is because if the U.S. Congress started to hand out statehoods, the Canadian province or region would have to wait in line for its turn. Puerto Rico and the District of Columbia (in which Washington D.C. is located) have both been in line for a long time and would demand first call. During all this time, the erstwhile Canadians would be relegated to the status of second-class U.S. citizens. The pity of it is that the present-day advocates of American annexation might have long since departed this life before their dreams could possibly be fulfilled.

In short, this hardly seems a satisfactory way out of Canada's constitutional dilemma.

SUMMARY

The various options discussed in this Chapter will no doubt arise in the course of Canada's constitutional talks. It is important that the terminology becomes familiar to Canadians.

13
WHAT IF QUÉBEC SEPARATES?

This is something which none of us wishes to contemplate. Nonetheless, it would be unwise not to analyze the implications.

Québec has made great strides in the past 30 years, socially and economically, within the framework of the Canadian federation. Its language and culture have been protected from total absorption in a predominantly English-speaking continent. Pressure for independence has fluctuated over the years but reached a crisis level following the collapse of the Meech Lake Accord in June 1990. A poll released on May 1, 1991 by Montréal's *La Presse* showed that 48 per cent of Québecers still favour sovereignty, but this figure represents a drop of 16 per cent (from 6 per cent) over the previous poll taken in November 1990. The separatist movement may have subsided somewhat, but it has the support of powerful groups such as the labour movement, the teachers' union, the youth wing of Premier Bourassa's Liberal Party, and the separatist Parti Québécois under Jacques Parizeau. Certainly, the situation remains very volatile and unpredictable.

IMPLICATIONS FOR QUÉBEC

Québec independence is expected to provoke a large exodus of its English-speaking population, which now makes up 12 per cent (800,000) of Québec's 6.8 million people. A poll taken in April 1991 showed that if separation takes place, 4 per cent of Québec anglophones plan to leave — a large proportion of these being young persons aged 18 to 24 years. This could be the beginning of the end of the English community in Québec.

Québec's financial structure would be affected. The province would no longer be entitled to federal transfer payments, which in 1988 exceeded the tax revenue which the federal government received from Québec.

For many Québecers, separation would mean loss of jobs in the federal civil service within the Ottawa area as well as federal jobs in government offices and in Crown corporations within Québec.

Nor would a sovereign Québec ever again have access to the military forces of Canada in the event of a crisis, such as the one that occurred at Oka in 1990.

Following separation Québec would have to negotiate its own free trade deal with the United States, since the present Agreement (which Québec strongly supported) would not automatically apply to Québec as a sovereign state. The disparity between Québec's six million people and the American population of 200 million would be far greater than that faced by Canada's 26 million people in negotiating the present Free Trade Agreement. If Québec were to negotiate a new deal, the United States would probably insist on changes being made to the existing Agreement (just as it is threatening to do now in tripartite negotiations with Mexico). American pressure is being exerted now to remove Canadian culture from the protection it now enjoys against the import of American culture — an area of particular sensitivity to Québecers. If the new terms demanded by Québec should prove too inflexible for Québec to tolerate, the result would be no new agreement at all, and no favoured trade relations with the United States. Furthermore, since the language of commerce is English, the Québec business community, which supports sovereignty, would be obliged to use English, not French, in its continental trade dealings.

Nor could Québecers assume that a vote for sovereignty would assure "sovereignty association" with Canada. Much would depend on how separation came about. It is highly unlikely that agreement could be reached amongst all the provinces and the federal government to a formal constitutional amendment allowing Québec to leave confederation. As a result, separation would likely be brought about by a unilateral declaration of independence by Québec. Following this, it could take years to complete a post-separation agreement, since discussions would not even begin until a new government structure was established, not only in Québec, but in the new Canada without Québec. It would be rare indeed for Canada at that point to share its banking system, currency, postal and other services, with a foreign country (Québec), or allow its Crown corporations to continue to operate in a separate Québec.

As Constitutional Affairs Minister Joe Clark said (speaking in Calgary on May 28, 1991), we can't come apart politically and come together economically.

Perhaps these realities will cause second thoughts for those who view Québec independence as a panacea.

IMPLICATIONS FOR CANADA

The Atlantic provinces would be physically separated from the rest of Canada. Ontario would dominate the new Canada with its population of 9 million in a new Canada of 20 million. A House of Commons would have almost half of its seats allotted to Ontario.

If Québec unilaterally declared independence (which it would have to do unless all governments agreed to its withdrawal), it could mean that the rest of Canada would be left with no constitutional structure. The present Constitution might be no longer applicable, prefaced as it is on Québec's presence in confederation. It could even mean that the existing government in Ottawa would have no mandate to act on behalf of a new Canada. Concerning such perilous matters, there are no guidelines or precedents. In the words of constitutional law professor Gerald L. Gall, of the University of Alberta: "This is basically unchartered constitutional terrain."

In contrast to Québec, which would have an independent government immediately in place and functioning, little planning appears to have been done to ensure the continued existence of the rest of Canada with its sprawling geography, nine provinces and two Territories. The federal government is in a difficult position: it must focus on keeping the country together, not on its possible dismemberment.

Yet it is only realistic to have an alternative plan, in the event of possible failure of the current constitutional talks. These and other thoughts were brought out by Alan C. Cairns, political scientist, University of British Columbia, in a research paper he presented at a symposium in Toronto in January 1991. He pointed out that following separation, the rest of Canada would have no constitutional existence, no institutional structure, no official spokesperson to speak to it, or for it, to define it, or debate its future. In his words, it could be "headless and faceless."[18]

---

[18] Papers presented at this symposium have been published by the University of Toronto Press under the title "Options Canada."

If constitutional negotiations fail and Québec decides to separate, it would (according to Bill 150 of the Québec National Assembly) become a sovereign nation within a year following the referendum. Such are the implications to Canada of Québec independence. It would also give rise to a number of contentious issues.

THE NATIONAL DEBT

In 1984, when the Mulroney government took office, the national debt was $180 billion. By 1991, it had more than doubled to $374 billion, with the annual operating deficit running around $30 billion. If Québec's separation occurred in 1993 (albeit regretfully), the national debt at that time would be approximately $400 billion. It should be noted that the national debt is held in the name of all Canadians.

Québec's share, if based on its proportion to the total population, would be 25 per cent, or $100 billion. If based on Québec's proportion of national assets, its share would be 18.5 per cent or $74 billion.

Whatever the amount — $74 billion or $100 billion — Québec would begin its new life as a sovereign nation with a very heavy indebtedness. To that would be added Québec's own provincial debt (which is said to be around $50 billion) and its 1991 projected fiscal deficit, estimated at $2 billion.

Presumably, Québec would pay off its share of the national debt by issuing new bonds. In its search for new foreign investors, Québec would be competing with many other countries such as Kuwait and Eastern European nations, which are currently clamoring for new capital. If investors became wary of Québec's future, Québec would have to pay a higher interest rate. Complicating the situation is the fact that foreigners already hold some $22 billion worth of Québec bonds, mostly arising out of Hydro–Québec developments. International finance experts say that if separation occurs, those investors would probably sell their bonds and seek reimbursement, creating a further strain on Québec's fiscal structure. Already (as of March 1991), Canadian Bond Rating Services put Québec bonds on a "credit alert."

All of these factors would complicate the problem of attracting and holding new investors, so essential to the survival of a new, small nation.

As for the rest of Canada, it would be left with a reduced national debt as a result of Québec assuming its share. Nevertheless, Canada's debt would remain substantial, and with the situation not greatly different from now. Canada's tax base however would be considerably larger than that of Québec.

It follows that if any province or region should decide to separate, it too would take with it a proportionate share of the national debt. Like Québec, it would launch its new autonomous status under a heavy debt load, which, among other things, would considerably reduce its attractiveness as a possible subject for American annexation.

DIVISION OF ASSETS

This poses an even greater difficulty than the national debt. No one knows the worth of federal assets across Canada.

The Treasury Department estimates that the federal government owns 21 million hectares of land and 30 million square metres of building space. Determining their value is impossible. In recent years, in the National Capital Region, many new federal buildings have been erected on the Québec side, including the fabulous Museum of Civilization.

One suggestion is that a balance be struck to equate Québec's share of federal assets outside Québec with Canada's share of federal assets within Québec. Achieving a settlement could require many years, and in the meantime there would be uncertainty as to who had responsibility for the preservation, care and maintenance of these costly assets.

SETTLEMENT OF BOUNDARIES

Many complicated factors would arise in determining the boundaries for a sovereign Québec.

In 1867, when Québec became a province, it was a boot-shaped strip of country along the St. Lawrence River with the toe pointing towards Ontario and the heel towards the northeastern United States.

In 1898, Québec was extended northward (as were Manitoba and Ontario). Québec's boundary then reached the lower corner of James Bay and extended northeast to what was later to become Labrador. In 1912, Parliament passed the "Québec Boundaries Extension Act." It provided that Québec's northern boundary would extend northward to include the District of Ungava, thus constituting the present area of Québec. That extension was subject to five conditions, one of which was that trusteeship of the Indians, and management of any land reserved for their use, shall remain with the government of Canada.

Since the 1912 extension of Québec's boundaries is the creation of an Act of the Canadian Parliament, an argument has been raised that these boundaries have no existence or authenticity outside of Canadian law. If any credence were given to this suggestion, it could mean that Québec's boundaries, on separation, could revert to those at the time of confederation.

Whatever the outcome, even if Québec separates, the government of Canada would still have substantial powers over the northern part of Québec by virtue of federal responsibility for the Indian population, and the proviso in the 1912 Act.

Northern Québec is inhabited almost entirely by Indians and a few Inuit. The Indians are mostly English-speaking. The Crees of James Bay have declared that if Québec separates, they want to remain in Canada, occupying their ancestral lands which they claim belong to them, not to either Canada or Québec. They argue that if Québec can separate from Canada, then parts of Québec can also separate from Québec. The Grand Council of the Crees, meeting on August 6, 1991, defined their options: go with Canada, go with Québec, or go it on their own.

Not only are the natives reviewing their position, but the Equality Party (an English minority group) is studying the possibility of creating an English enclave within a sovereign Québec. With different groups considering "separation from a separating Québec," the boundary issue becomes more complicated.

Whatever the final settlement, Canada would have to insist on the creation of a corridor south of the St. Lawrence River to provide a link between Ontario and the Maritimes.

HYDRO-QUÉBEC

No discussion of Québec, whether autonomous or part of Canada, would be complete without an understanding of the significance of Hydro-Québec. This arm of the Québec government has developed massive hydroelectric projects in northern Québec which are regarded as linchpins of Québec's economic future.

Hydro-Québec consists of two major projects. The first, James Bay I, began in 1971 during Robert Bourassa's first term as Premier of Québec, and was completed in 1984 at a cost of $13.7 billion — on which the province still carries a substantial debt load. It consists of an elaborate system of dams, dikes and power-generating plants erected on La Grande River which flows into James Bay. Vast areas of land, which had for centuries been home to the Cree Indians, were flooded. Natives tried to stop its construction through legal action, but lost. As a consequence, in 1975 they signed the "James Bay and Northern Québec Agreement," which gave them $135 million in compensation, as well as land and other rights. The natives now claim that as a result of this development, the waterways have been polluted with toxic effluents, particularly methyl mercury, and that fish, the staple food of the Cree and Inuit, have been contaminated.

The second of Hydro-Québec's projects, known as James Bay II, is now in the early stages of development. It will completely re-route five rivers and cause massive flooding. The first phase is to consist of two hydroelectric plants on the Great Whale river system, with construction beginning in 1993 and scheduled for completion in 1998 at a cost of $12.8 billion. The Crees, now richer and wiser, have launched several legal challenges, and along with environmentalists, have delayed commencement of construction. The Crees claim that the Hydro-Québec development will ruin their traditional hunting grounds, and by opening up their isolated communities to the outside world it will destroy their way of life. They have even taken their complaints to United Nations hearings in Geneva.

The second phase of James Bay II will involve construction of 116 additional dams on two other rivers in northern Québec at a cost of $16 billion, to be completed by the year 2007. The magnitude of these projects is without parallel in the history of Canadian Construction industry.

In 1989, Hydro-Québec entered into a tentative contract with the New York Power Authority for the supply of hydroelectricity, beginning in 1995 and extending over 21 years and worth $17 billion. A similar contract with the State of Vermont is valued at $8 billion. These contracts can be re-opened at any time up to November 30, 1991. Both these states, which are committed to environmental protection, are now raising concerns with the Québec government since some of the power will eventually come from the controversial Great Whale project. Mayor David Dinkins of New York City has even questioned the size of the contracts in the light of declining energy needs due to improved conservation. Thus these huge contracts, on which Hydro-Québec depends and which appeared so promising two years ago, have become a subject of considerable controversy. Finally, the Quebec Environment Minister, yielding to international pressure, announced on August 21, 1991 that construction on the Great Whale project would be delayed until a thorough environmental assessment is made. In a later statement, Premier Bourassa announced that the entire project would be delayed for a year.

Meanwhile, in order to encourage greater consumption of electric power, Hydro-Québec is granting huge incentives, in the form of cheap electricity to multinational companies, to establish aluminum smelters in the St. Lawrence industrial area. For the decade of the '90s, Québec has budgeted over $24 billion for hydro-development, yet in 1990 it recorded a loss of $125 million in sales. Critics say there is neither the demand nor the need for electric power on the magnitude of these developments. Nevertheless, Québec is speculating on the success of these projects as the guarantee of its future economic security.

SUMMARY

Québec separation could be a lengthy and contentious process. It would create colossal problems for both Québec and the rest of Canada, including settlement of major issues — dividing the national debt, sharing the national assets, settling Québec's boundaries, protecting native interests — as well as the need to design a new constitutional and political structure for Canada without Québec. The whole process would cause a profound disruption to our national life.

14 SUMMARY AND CONCLUSION

WHERE WE STAND NOW

Québec has demanded a massive transfer of powers from the federal government. Unless it receives an acceptable and binding proposal from Canada, it will hold a referendum on sovereignty by October 1992.

The federal government is to release its Proposal for Constitutional Reform in mid-September. This proposal has been the work of federal government officials and of the "National Unity Committee," consisting of 18 Conservative Cabinet Ministers under Constitutional Affairs Minister Joe Clark. All of their discussions were held in secret. (For further particulars, see pages 63, 68.)

A Joint Parliamentary Committee, consisting of 10 Senators and 20 MPs, will conduct hearings on the Proposal throughout Canada over a period of four months, beginning in September 1991. In February 1992, it will present a Plan for a Renewed Canada, which will apparently be the federal government's final proposal. To be binding, as Québec has demanded, it will require approval by Parliament and by the number of provincial legislatures stipulated in the Constitution (explained above on page 20). If the plan is accepted by Québec, the October 1992 referendum, if held, could be on federalism, rather than on sovereignty. If a referendum vote approved of sovereignty, the Québec government could seek independence one year from that date.

This is where we stand as at August 15, 1991.

WHERE WE SEEM TO BE GOING

As of the date of writing (August 15, 1991), the federal government's Proposal for Constitutional Reform has not been released; hence, there must be an element of speculation in these remarks, requiring adjustments as events unfold.

Two aspects need to be examined here: the direction of constitutional change; and the process by which it is being achieved.

Québec's two major demands regarding constitutional reform are for recognition of its distinct society status, and for vastly increased provincial powers. Present indications are that both demands will be met in some form and to some extent.

In all likelihood, the term "distinct society" will reappear in the new federal Proposal, though perhaps under a different name, such as Québec's "unique society" or "distinct character" — the purpose being to avoid association with the controversial Meech Lake Accord. Whatever the language, the problem remains of how to define the term, how to phrase it, or where to place it in the Constitution.

If greater legislative are granted to Québec alone, it would create provincial inequality; if granted to all provinces, it would result in radical decentralization, which could weaken the central government and undermine its effectiveness as a unifying force for holding the country together. (For further explanation, see pages 103, 105-107.)

Bilingualism will likely cease to be official government policy, except for bilingual services in Federal departments and agencies. This would be in keeping with recommendations of the Spicer Commission.

Both Senate reform and aboriginal concerns require further study before consensus can be achieved. Therefore, any proposed changes may receive little more than approval in principle. (Explained further on pages 72-80, 91-98.)

Perhaps the most contentious issue will be division of powers between the provincial and federal governments. On August 20, 1991, Constitutional Affairs Minister Joe Clark hinted that the federal Proposal would include a recommendation fro the establishment of a "Council of Federation." It would be formed to deal with jurisdictional disputes between the two levels of government. It would be a third federal chamber in addition to the House of Commons and a reformed Senate. The provinces would appoint or elect their representatives. Presumably, if agreement could be reached in this body concerning federal-provincial disputes, a constitutional amendment would not be required each time a change was made.

The Québec representatives on the Unity Cabinet Committee temporarily left the meeting when the matter was discussed, out of concern the proposal could undermine their provincial autonomy. It is too early to assess the merits of this proposal, but Canadians will wish to follow developments as further details become available.

As to the process for achieving reform, secrecy surrounded the discussions amongst politicians and federal civil servants during the months of discussions that preceded release of the government's proposal in September 1991. Despite the fact that this group met regularly over a lengthy period, Canadians were given no information as to what matters were under discussion. (See above at pages 63, 68.)

As to public participation in the process, no representatives of the general public were on the National Committee (which formulated the federal Proposal) nor were there to be any on the Joint Parliamentary Committee (which would finalize the federal Plan). Unless full public hearings are held during this process, the transition from Proposal to Plan could be perceived as being dominated by politicians. For this reason alone, Canadians could properly insist on a national referendum before approval of any final constitutional package. At the Beaudoin Edwards Committee hearings, strong public support was expressed for the use of a national referendum and a constituent assembly as a process for amending the Constitution. (For a detailed explanation, see pages 61-63, 99-102.)

As time passes, there could be risk as well of political manipulation. Once again Canada is tied to a deadline — this time created by the Québec government with its threat of an October 1992 referendum. As that deadline approaches, the country could again find itself immersed in an atmosphere of crisis (real or concocted) with the choice between acceptance of the federal Plan or risking Québec separation. The tactic could in fact be part of the federal government's re-election strategy. (Further explained on pages 70-71.)

In the months ahead, Canadians should continue to scrutinize the constitutional process in order to ensure openness, more citizen involvement and avoidance of pressure tactics and manipulation.

WHAT CANADIANS SEEM TO WANT

Canadians generally want every effort to be expended in convincing Québec that its future lies within the Canadian federation. At the same time, they would wish any constitutional arrangement to ensure the preservation of an effective government for all Canada. They would not wish that accommodating Québec now, in order to avoid separation, would simply lead to further demands for more powers in future. There is a feeling in Canada that many pressing domestic decisions have been already too long delayed because of the nation's preoccupation with constitutional concerns. It is only reasonable to demand that any settlement reached now would be relatively permanent and not open to periodic re-negotiation.

On specific issues, such as distinct society status for Québec, Canadians should not object to a clause in the Constitution recognizing Québec's distinctiveness. The only proviso must be that the promotion of Québec's distinct character must not infringe on the fundamental rights and freedoms of minorities living within its borders. This would require that the Canadian Charter of Rights and Freedoms take precedence over the "distinct society" clause — a condition to which Québec would not agree at the time of the Meech Lake debate. It is only proper that Canadians have responsibility to protect citizens wherever they live.

Some groups have suggested that the distinct society clause be balanced by a so-called "Canada clause" which would give recognition to certain fundamental characteristics of Canada, such as its cultural diversity, its aboriginal heritage and its English-French duality. Such a clause for the preamble to the Constitution was suggested at the time of Meech Lake, but was rejected.

On the subject of bilingualism, if jurisdiction over language is transferred to the provinces, there would no longer be a nationwide duty to provide bilingual services. If, for example, some provinces chose not to support minority language education, then francophone minorities living outside Québec and English minorities in Québec would find their language privileges curtailed. (For a full discussion of bilingualism, see pages 80-86.)

The Spicer Commission Report probably reflects the views of most Canadians on the subject of multiculturalism, namely that government funding for ethnic groups should be diverted to improved orientation services for new Canadians. (Discussed further on pages 86-88.)

Senate reform remains obscure and confusing to many Canadians. (Fully discussed on pages 72-80.) A similar reaction pertains to aboriginal issues: when Canadians repeatedly told the Spicer Commission that they lacked even a basic understanding of the subject. (See pages 91-98 for a detailed analysis of native issues.)

In regard to both Senate reform and aboriginal concerns, much more study and discussions are needed as well as opportunities for the public to become involved — as indeed they must, since both matters are of vital importance to the future of Canada. Unless some level of unanimity is achieved, most Canadians would consider it premature to have a position entrenched in the Constitution. The resolution of both these issues requires an effective national government with a commitment to these causes, since groups advocating reform sense considerable urgency. At the same time, by their very nature, these are not subjects which lend themselves to speedy solutions.

Of all subjects, decentralization is viewed by most Canadians as the greatest threat to Canadian federalism. It is frequently stated in the media that all provinces want more powers. The fact is that the premiers of only a very few provinces (notably Alberta and Québec) take that position. Incidentally, in the case of Alberta, this position is not supported by Alberta citizens (see page 105). The majority of the Canadian people, the majority of the provinces and most of the provincial premiers have assigned high priority to a strong central government. Yet decentralization is undoubtedly the direction of current constitutional negotiations. Though some shift in powers between the two levels of government is appropriate because of changing circumstances, Canadians would want a clear limit on the extent of that transfer and the resulting weakened effectiveness of the central government.

It is not the task of this writer to delineate a division of legislative powers between the provinces and the federal government. Suffice to say, whatever is done should be done in the interests of all Canadians and not for political expediency.

In assessing the future, Canadians on the whole are reasonable and flexible in their expectations, but their highest priority is towards the preservation and maintenance of a strong united country.

HOW CAN WE HELP CANADA?

We can help Canada by adding to our knowledge of the issues facing the country, by being positive in our thinking and constructive in our outlook.

We can help Canada by intelligently assessing the options available, thus having a small share in the future direction of the country.

We can help Canada by being watchful of the process being followed in effecting change, and by insisting on honesty and openness on the part of public officials and on the appropriate level of public participation.

We can help Canada by supporting the efforts of Constitutional Affairs Minister Joe Clark, and trusting him to reflect the will of the Canadian people.

We can help Canada by being idealistic, yet at the same time, realistic.

Canadians have a right to ask whether the granting of additional powers to Québec now will mean the end of further demands, or merely a postponement, not the elimination of Québec's separatist ambitions.

Canadians have a right to insist that this country, built by our forebears and with over a century of history, shall not be fractured or fragmented by the political ambitions of those in power.

We can help Canada by never abandoning our primary goal — to design a new Constitution and institutional structure acceptable to Québec and fair to all Canada.

But if we should fail and Québec chooses to leave confederation (regrettable though that would be), the rest of Canada must have ready an alternative plan (even as Québec already has) for restructuring — to ensure that the nine provinces and two Territories, which would constitute the new Canadian federation, would remain intact, united, vibrant and cohesive. Planning is needed now so that the devastating loss of Québec would not lead to the disintegration of the rest of Canada.

While continuing to work steadfastly for an undivided Canada, we will nevertheless have planned realistically for an eventuality which we hope will never happen. That can be our way of sharing responsibility for the future.

CONCLUDING COMMENTS

The purpose of this book is not to give answers, but to provide facts on which people can find answers for themselves.

This is not the only book that should be read, and not the only book that should be written.

Its purpose is to bring the discussion of Canada's future to the level of ordinary citizens — the young, the old and the in-betweens — rather than restricting it to academics, entrepreneurs and politicians — important though these may be.

It is the people of Canada who should be deciding the future of Canada — not necessarily by direct involvement, because it is a highly technical subject — but rather by Canadians telling leaders in general terms what they want done, and how they want it done.

The book is offered in the hope that all people can share in the pleasures and the pain , the challenges and the responsibilities, of the next chapter of Canadian history.

ABOUT THE AUTHOR

MARJORIE MONTGOMERY BOWKER was born on Prince Edward Island and raised in Alberta. She graduated in law, was admitted to the Alberta bar, and in 1966 was appointed Judge of the Provincial Court of Alberta, Family and Juvenile Divisions, a position she held for 17 years. Since retiring in 1983, she has devoted much of her time to national issues. Her first two books — on the Free Trade Agreement in 1988 and on the Meech Lake Accord in 1990 — were national best sellers. Two of the tributes she most enjoyed came from a pioneer woman doctor in the north who said, "I couldn't believe they had been written by a lawyer," and from a lady in Saskatchewan who said, "You made us think."

She has been the recipient of many honours: an honorary Doctor of Laws degree from a women's university in Korea in 1968; the Queen's Silver Jubilee medal in 1978; the Alberta Achievement Award in 1981; the Award of Merit from the American Association of Conciliation Courts in 1983; and in 1989 was named Woman of the Year by the Edmonton Business and Professional Women's Club, received a "Tribute to Women" Award from the YWCA of Edmonton, and the Distinguished Canadian Award from the Council of Canadians in Ottawa; two further honorary degrees would follow in 1991.

Her husband, Wilbur F. Bowker, now retired, was Dean of the Faculty of Law at the University of Alberta for 20 years, and later, founding Director of the Alberta Law Reform Institute. In October 1990 they both received the Order of Canada. It is very unusual for a husband and wife to be so honoured at the same time and for different reasons. That same year they celebrated their 50th wedding anniversary. Their three grown children and their spouses are all in the health care field — living in Edmonton, Alberta; in Hamilton, Ontario; and in North Bay, Ontario. There are seven grandchildren.

**Other Books from Lone Pine Publishing of interest to Canadians
from Coast to Coast**

INSIDE OUTER CANADA

by David Kilgour

A look at the political and financial discrimination felt by the regions of Canada
outside the Golden Triangle of Toronto, Ottawa and Montreal.

$14.95 softcover   256 pp.   5 1/2 x 8 1/2   ISBN 0-919433-86-3

UNEASY PATRIOTS

by David Kilgour

An historical and personal overview of Western Canada's place in confederation

$12.95 softcover   272 pp.   5 1/2 x 8 1/2   ISBN 0-919433-53-7

BATTLING THE BAY:

The Turn-of-the-Century Adventures of Fur Trader Ed Nagle

by Jordan Zinovich

The story of the man who outfoxed the Hudson's Bay Fur Company from Edmont
to the Great Slave Lake.

$14.95 softcover   288 pp   5 1/2 x 8 1/2   ISBN 0-919433-96-0

Available Fall '91

THE PROSPECTOR: NORTH OF 60

by Ted Nagle and Jordan Zinovich

Personal anecdote, adventure and intrigue fill this book on one man's role in the ra
for ownership of the North's mineral resources.

$22.95 hardcover   288 pp   5 1/2 x 8 1/2   ISBN 0-919433-67-7
$14.95 softcover   288 pp   5 1/2 x 8 1/2   ISBN 0-919433-61-8

YUKON CHALLENGE

by John Firth

The story of one of the most guelling races held anywhere in the world —
the 1600-kilometre Yukon Quest International Sled Dog Race.

$12.95 softcover   240 pp.   5 1/2 x 8 1/2   ISBN 0-919433-85-5

Look for these books at your local book store. If unavailable, order direct from
Lone Pine Publishing, 206, 10426-81 Ave, Edmonton, Alberta T6E 1X5
Phone: (403) 433-9333 Fax: (403) 433 9646